Lecture Notes in Economics and Mathematical Systems

(Vol. 1–15: Lecture Notes in Operations Research and Mathematical Economics, Vol. 16–59: Lecture Notes in Operations Research and Mathematical Systems)

Vol. 1: H. Bühlmann, H. Loeffel, E. Nievergelt, Einführung in die Theorie und Praxis der Entscheidung bei Unsicherheit. 2. Auflage, IV, 125 Seiten. 1969.

Vol. 2: U. N. Bhat, A Study of the Queueing Systems M/G/1 and GI/M/1. VIII, 78 pages. 1968.

Vol. 3: A. Strauss, An Introduction to Optimal Control Theory. Out of print

Vol. 4: Branch and Bound: Eine Einführung. 2., geänderte Auflage. Herausgegeben von F. Weinberg. VII, 174 Seiten. 1973.

Vol. 5: L. P. Hyvärinen, Information Theory for Systems Engineers. VII, 205 pages. 1968.

Vol. 6: H. P. Künzi, O. Müller, E. Nievergelt, Einführungskursus in die dynamische Programmierung. IV, 103 Seiten. 1968.

Vol. 7: W. Popp, Einführung in die Theorie der Lagerhaltung. VI, 173 Seiten. 1968.

Vol. 8: J. Teghem, J. Loris-Teghem, J. P. Lambotte, Modèles d'Attente M/G/1 et GI/M/1 à Arrivées et Services en Groupes. III, 53 pages. 1969.

Vol. 9: E. Schultze, Einführung in die mathematischen Grundlagen der Informationstheorie. VI, 116 Seiten. 1969.

Vol. 10: D. Hochstädter, Stochastische Lagerhaltungsmodelle. VI, 269 Seiten. 1969.

Vol. 11/12: Mathematical Systems Theory and Economics. Edited by H. W. Kuhn and G. P. Szegö. VIII, III, 486 pages. 1969.

Vol. 13: Heuristische Planungsmethoden. Herausgegeben von F. Weinberg und C. A. Zehnder. II, 93 Seiten. 1969.

Vol. 14: Computing Methods in Optimization Problems. V, 191 pages. 1969.

Vol. 15: Economic Models, Estimation and Risk Programming: Essays in Honor of Gerhard Tintner. Edited by K. A. Fox, G. V. L. Narasimham and J. K. Sengupta. VIII, 461 pages. 1969.

Vol. 16: H. P. Künzi und W. Oettli, Nichtlineare Optimierung: Neuere Verfahren, Bibliographie. IV, 180 Seiten. 1969.

Vol. 17: H. Bauer und K. Neumann, Berechnung optimaler Steuerungen, Maximumprinzip und dynamische Optimierung. VIII, 188 Seiten. 1969.

Vol. 18: M. Wolff, Optimale Instandhaltungspolitiken in einfachen Systemen. V, 143 Seiten. 1970.

Vol. 19: L. P. Hyvärinen, Mathematical Modeling for Industrial Processes. VI, 122 pages. 1970.

Vol. 20: G. Uebe, Optimale Fahrpläne. IX, 161 Seiten. 1970.

Vol. 21: Th. M. Liebling, Graphentheorie in Planungs- und Tourenproblemen am Beispiel des städtischen Straßendienstes. IX, 118 Seiten. 1970.

Vol. 22: W. Eichhorn, Theorie der homogenen Produktionsfunktion. VIII, 119 Seiten. 1970.

Vol. 23: A. Ghosal, Some Aspects of Queueing and Storage Systems. IV, 93 pages. 1970.

Vol. 24: G. Feichtinger, Lernprozesse in stochastischen Automaten. V, 66 Seiten. 1970.

Vol. 25: R. Henn und O. Opitz, Konsum- und Produktionstheorie I. II, 124 Seiten. 1970.

Vol. 26: D. Hochstädter und G. Uebe, Ökonometrische Methoden. XII, 250 Seiten. 1970.

Vol. 27: I. H. Mufti, Computational Methods in Optimal Control Problems. IV, 45 pages. 1970.

Vol. 28: Theoretical Approaches to Non-Numerical Problem Solving. Edited by R. B. Banerji and M. D. Mesarovic. VI, 466 pages. 1970.

Vol. 29: S. E. Elmaghraby, Some Network Models in Management Science. III, 176 pages. 1970.

Vol. 30: H. Noltemeier, Sensitivitätsanalyse bei diskreten linearen Optimierungsproblemen. VI, 102 Seiten. 1970.

Vol. 31: M. Kühlmeyer, Die nichtzentrale t-Verteilung. II, 106 Seiten. 1970.

Vol. 32: F. Bartholomes und G. Hotz, Homomorphismen und Reduktionen linearer Sprachen. XII, 143 Seiten. 1970. DM 18,–

Vol. 33: K. Hinderer, Foundations of Non-stationary Dynamic Programming with Discrete Time Parameter. VI, 160 pages. 1970.

Vol. 34: H. Störmer, Semi-Markoff-Prozesse mit endlich vielen Zuständen. Theorie und Anwendungen. VII, 128 Seiten. 1970.

Vol. 35: F. Ferschl, Markovketten. VI, 168 Seiten. 1970.

Vol. 36: M. J. P. Magill, On a General Economic Theory of Motion. VI, 95 pages. 1970.

Vol. 37: H. Müller-Merbach, On Round-Off Errors in Linear Programming. V, 48 pages. 1970.

Vol. 38: Statistische Methoden I. Herausgegeben von E. Walter. VIII, 338 Seiten. 1970.

Vol. 39: Statistische Methoden II. Herausgegeben von E. Walter. IV, 157 Seiten. 1970.

Vol. 40: H. Drygas, The Coordinate-Free Approach to Gauss-Markov Estimation. VIII, 113 pages. 1970.

Vol. 41: U. Ueing, Zwei Lösungsmethoden für nichtkonvexe Programmierungsprobleme. IV, 92 Seiten. 1971.

Vol. 42: A. V. Balakrishnan, Introduction to Optimization Theory in a Hilbert Space. IV, 153 pages. 1971.

Vol. 43: J. A. Morales, Bayesian Full Information Structural Analysis. VI, 154 pages. 1971.

Vol. 44: G. Feichtinger, Stochastische Modelle demographischer Prozesse. IX, 404 Seiten. 1971.

Vol. 45: K. Wendler, Hauptaustauschschritte (Principal Pivoting). II, 64 Seiten. 1971.

Vol. 46: C. Boucher, Leçons sur la théorie des automates mathématiques. VIII, 193 pages. 1971.

Vol. 47: H. A. Nour Eldin, Optimierung linearer Regelsysteme mit quadratischer Zielfunktion. VIII, 163 Seiten. 1971.

Vol. 48: M. Constam, FORTRAN für Anfänger. 2. Auflage. VI, 148 Seiten. 1973.

Vol. 49: Ch. Schneeweiß, Regelungstechnische stochastische Optimierungsverfahren. XI, 254 Seiten. 1971.

Vol. 50: Unternehmensforschung Heute – Übersichtsvorträge der Züricher Tagung von SVOR und DGU, September 1970. Herausgegeben von M. Beckmann. IV, 133 Seiten. 1971.

Vol. 51: Digitale Simulation. Herausgegeben von K. Bauknecht und W. Nef. IV, 207 Seiten. 1971.

Vol. 52: Invariant Imbedding. Proceedings 1970. Edited by R. E. Bellman and E. D. Denman. IV, 148 pages. 1971.

Vol. 53: J. Rosenmüller, Kooperative Spiele und Märkte. III, 152 Seiten. 1971.

Vol. 54: C. C. von Weizsäcker, Steady State Capital Theory. III, 102 pages. 1971.

Vol. 55: P. A. V. B. Swamy, Statistical Inference in Random Coefficient Regression Models. VIII, 209 pages. 1971.

Vol. 56: Mohamed A. El-Hodiri, Constrained Extrema. Introduction to the Differentiable Case with Economic Applications. III, 130 pages. 1971.

Vol. 57: E. Freund, Zeitvariable Mehrgrößensysteme. VIII,160 Seiten. 1971.

Vol. 58: P. B. Hagelschuer, Theorie der linearen Dekomposition. VII, 191 Seiten. 1971.

continuation on page 121

Lecture Notes
in Economics and
Mathematical Systems
Managing Editors: M. Beckmann and H. P. Künzi

Mathematical Economics

135

Hanjiro Haga

A Disequilibrium–Equilibrium Model with Money and Bonds

A Keynesian–Walrasian Synthesis

Springer-Verlag
Berlin · Heidelberg · New York 1976

Author
Prof. Dr. Hanjiro Haga
Department of Economics
Tohoku University
Kawauchi
Sendai, 980/Japan

Library of Congress Cataloging in Publication Data

Haga, Hanjirō, 1924-
A disequilibrium-equilibrium model with money and bonds.

(Lecture notes in economics and mathematical systems ; 135 : Mathematical economics)
Includes bibliographical references and index.
1. Equilibrium (Economics)--Mathematical models.
2. Economics--Mathematical models. I. Title.
II. Series: Lecture notes in economics and mathematical systems ; 135.
HB145.H3 330'.01'8 76-49470

AMS Subject Classifikations (1970): 90A15, 90A99

ISBN 978-3-540-07992-7 ISBN 978-3-642-48148-2 (eBook)
DOI 10.1007/978-3-642-48148-2

Acknowledgments

This monograph is an expansion of my discussion paper [8]. After I wrote the discussion paper, I found that several questions remained. I took these up with Professors M. Otsuki, H. Hori, and O. Kamoike, of Tohoku University, whose comments were most helpful. Also, I often discussed the paper with two graduate students, Mr. R. Okumura, now at Hirosaki University, and with Mr. H. Sato, who is at Tohoku University. If the present monograph is an improvement over the discussion paper, I am greatly indebted to these colleagues and students. Thanks are also due to Mr. E. Notar and Mrs. H. Kotake for English language editorial assistance. I would like to express my appreciation to Prof. R. Sato, of Brown University, for the help he gave me in the process of publication; and to Prof. G.S. Suzawa, of the University of Rhode Island, for contributing many useful comments. Finally, I wish to express my thanks to the many typists, including Miss K. Kayaba, Mrs. S. Takahashi, and my daughter, who faced a difficult task, but did it well. Needless to say, the responsibility for any errors is mine alone.

TABLE OF CONTENTS

CHAPTER I

INTRODUCTION

In an article[1] in the *Review of Economic Studies*, Glustoff attempts to prove the existence of a Keynesian "equilibrium". The significance of his article transcends its explicit purpose of proving existence, since it deals with the more fundamental question of what is the nature of a Keynesian equilibrium with involuntary unemployment.[2] Moreover, it approaches the problem from an unorthodox point of view. Glustoff follows the direction of Clower,[3] who in turn goes back to Morishima[4] and Patinkin;[5] that is, unlike the theory based on *ex ante* demand or supply functions, he redefines the labour supply function using a "dual-decision hypothesis".

The root of this problem can be traced back to the classical discussion of *ex ante* and *ex post* by Ohlin,[6] the representative of the Stockholm school. Therefore one can say that Glustoff refines this line of discussion by utilizing a recent development in economics. One can also say that his approach is basically the same as that of Leijonhufvud who advocates the "Economics of Keynes" and not the "Keynesian Economics".

To explain Glustoff's discussion, let us begin with the following figures for convenience.

---

1. See [4].
2. See [13].
3. See [2].
4. See [15]. pp. 24-26.
5. See [21] and [22] (ch. 13 and ch. 14).
6. See [19].

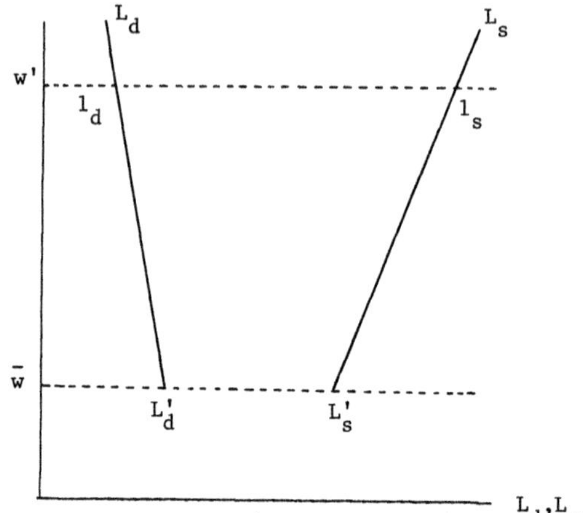

Fig. 1

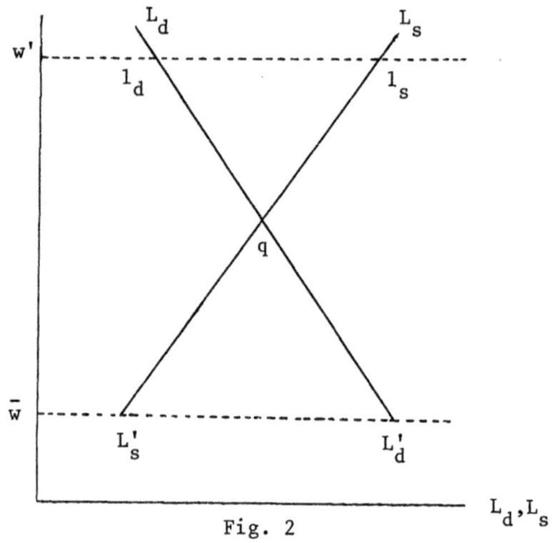

Fig. 2

In both of these figures, L_dL_d' and L_sL_s' represent the standard (or *ex ante*) demand and supply curves of labour. The vertical axis measures the wage rate; the horizontal axis measures the quantity of labour; and $\bar{w}$ is the "minimum wage" below which wages cannot fall due to social customs or government legislation.

Glustoff's argument is as follows. At w' in both Figures 1 and 2, the *ex ante* labour supply exceeds the *ex ante* labour demand. Accordingly, we have $l_s - l_d$ of excess *ex ante* labour supply which cannot be realized and therefore cannot be effective. That is, it is not actually employed, and hence the income from this part of the labour supply cannot "actually" be earned. Taking these circumstances into account, the labourers reexamine their utility maximization procedures, and ultimately decide to supply the realizable quantity $w'l_d$, instead of the *ex ante* quantity $w'l_s$. With the income gained by actually supplying $w'l_d$, this revised utility maximization procedure also determines the demand for goods. This is the "dual-decision hypothesis". In the *ex ante* approach, labour supply ($w'l_s$ in Figures 1 and 2) is determined simultaneously with the demand for other goods, such that utility is maximized regardless of whether this quantity of labour is actually employed. Under the "dual-decision hypothesis", the quantity of labour is, in the presence of excess supply, restricted to and determined by the labour demand of firms.[7] Thus, the effective and realizable income and the demand for other goods are determined simultaneously so as to maximize utility.

Glustoff constructs his model paying close attention to the following two stylized facts. First, in the case of an excess supply of labour, the firm possesses the power of decision over the quantity of labour to be actually employed, and labourers respond passively to the firm's decision. Second, the wage rate is inflexible downward and has a certain positive level below which it cannot fall. The way he treats these facts in his model is not *ad hoc*. According to the "dual-decision hypothesis", when the *ex ante* labour supply exceeds the *ex ante* labour demand, the labourers decide to supply exactly the quantity demanded and not less, because their utility is as high as possible when they offer as much labour as can be employed at the given wage rate. This, of course, means that the increase in

7. As was mentioned before, the underlying idea of the dual-decision hypothesis was already seen earlier in Morishima [15]. Moreover, one can find a similar idea in Patinkin [21] pp. 314-315. Morishima and Patinkin, however, did not analyse the dual-decision hypothesis in terms of maximization behaviour; it was Glustoff who first did this.

utility arising from the increase in income (which permits a higher level of expenditure on consumption goods) is larger than the increase in disutility arising from the corresponding sacrifice of leisure. This is the implication of Glustoff's Lemma 1 which is derived from certain plausible assumptions.[8]

The advantage of Glustoff's theorem is that he not only defines the state of involuntary unemployment using the "dual-decision hypothesis", but that he also demonstrates that the labour supply determined by such a decision process is a result of a certain type of optimization behaviour. The importance of Glustoff's work lies also in his analysis of the Keynesian equilibrium system as "another kind" of general equilibrium system containing many product markets and the money market as well as the labour market. The reason why we refer to Glustoff's model as "another kind" of general equilibrium system is that, although the labour market is in disequilibrium in the orthodox sense (because the *ex ante* demand and supply are not equal), it still possesses the essential properties of general equilibrium. The demand and supply finally determined are always equal, and all the individuals are in subjective equilibrium in the sense that the finally determined or realized demand and supply are both results of a kind of optimization behaviour.

There are, however, more than a few problems in Glustoff's treatment. First, he formulates labourers' optimization behaviour through the "dual-decision hypothesis" only in terms of labourers <u>as a whole</u> and not in terms of <u>each individual</u> labourer. Second, in his treatment of Keynesian equilibrium, there still exists the possibility of excess labour supply at the minimum wage. As long as the "dual-decision hypothesis" is assumed, this possibility should not exist. Thus Glustoff is not successful in proving the existence of a <u>Keynesian equilibrium</u>. In fact, in Lemma 2, which is particularly important for Glustoff's existence proof, a non-negative excess demand function for labour is assumed because of the "dual-decision hypothesis", and therefore the existence of positive excess supply of labour in the <u>Keynesian equilibrium</u> is incorrect.[9] Third, according to Glustoff, the minimum wage

---

8. See the assumption (U.a) and (U.b), and Lemma 1 in Glustoff [4] pp. 329-330.

9. See Glustoff [4] p. 334.

is given independently of other prices. But is this plausible? Even if it appears to be determined by non-economic forces, is it not actually determined by the government and labour unions with other prices being taken into account? Fourth, the demand or supply functions of households and firms are simply assumed to be singlevalued and continuous. But, this has to be questioned because the utility function in his model has the possibility of generating multi-valued demand and supply functions.[10] Fifth, his model does not consider the firm's profit maximization behaviour and, as a result, does not consider the firm's supply function of goods. Sixth, although his model contains money, he does not grasp the important property of money as the general means of exchange; that is, that only money can buy goods. Seventh, Glustoff's treatment of bonds is insufficient and does not really distinguish them from other goods. No mention is made of the demand (or supply) functions for either money or bonds. Along with understanding the character of money and bonds, it is desirable to introduce the demand or supply functions of these assets, based upon the optimization behaviours of the households and firms. In essence, although Glustoff's reconsideration of Keynes' under-employment equilibrium system from his own theoretical viewpoint can be considered an important contribution, we do not think that he has succeeded in synthesizing the Keynesian system with the Walrasian system. This is due to the fact that his way of introducing the goods, labour, money, and bond markets into the Walrasian general equilibrium system is inappropriate.

In this monograph we intend to construct a new equilibrium model by combining these two systems, accepting Clower's and Glustoff's re-interpretation of Keynes, and taking into account the seven points mentioned above. Our model consists of the product markets, money market, and bond market, together with the labour market, and adopts the dual-decision hypothesis. We start not from the total demand and supply functions, but from the individual demand and supply functions. We intend to clarify the structure and other properties of these functions. After constructing the model, we will try to prove the existence of a general equilibrium under the dual-decision hypothesis.

---

10. See Glustoff [4] pp. 328-329.

CHAPTER II

HOUSEHOLDS AND FIRMS

Our model is a system in which the wage is downwardly rigid. It has an intertemporal planning horizon; that is, its planning horizon runs over multiple periods.[11] Thus it is a kind of dynamic model. Since money is assumed to be the general means of exchange, the model has money constraints in addition to the budget constraints. Bonds will also be treated rather carefully since they introduce some problems hitherto overlooked.

1. The Household

There are two kinds of households in our model: labourers and rentiers.

1.1 Notation

The households belonging to the labour group are denoted by 1,2, ..., h, and the households belonging to the rentier group are denoted by h+1, h+2, ..., ℓ. The number of goods (including labour, money and bonds) is n+2. Money is denoted by 0, labour by 1, and bonds by n+1.

x_t^i : an n-dimensional column vector which denotes the i-th household's demand for goods in the t-th period.

$x_{t,j}^i$: the j-th element of x_t^i, namely, the demand for the j-th good. $x_{t,1}^i$ represents the net demand or net supply of labour. If $x_{t,1}^i$ is negative, it indicates the net supply of labour.

$\bar{x}_o^i$: an n-dimensional column vector which denotes the i-th household's initial holdings of goods in the 0-th period.

$x_{t,n+1}^i$: a scalar which denotes the i-th household's net demand (in the case where $x_{t,n+1}^i \geqq 0$) or net supply (in the case where $x_{t,n+1}^i < 0$) of

---

11. For example, the model in Haga [7]pp. 3-27 is one with an intertemporal planning horizon. It covers firms as well as households, but has the limitation that the budget constraints need a special assumption.

bonds. On each bond it is written that the holder can receive one dollar in the next period. If $x^i_{t,n+1}$ is negative, the i-th household must pay one dollar $\times \mid x^i_{t,n+1} \mid$.[12]

$x^i_{t,o}$: the i-th household's *ex ante* demand for money stock at the end of the t-th period.

$\bar{x}^i_{o,o}$: the i-th household's initial holding of money stock at the beginning of the 0-th period.

$\bar{x}^i_{o,j}$: $\bar{x}^i_{o,j}$ is the j-th element of the vector $\bar{x}^i_o$ which denotes the i-th household's initial holding of the j-th good, excluding labour, bonds and money stock (j=2,3, ..., n).

P_o : an n-dimensional row vector denoting the money prices of goods (excluding bonds and money) in the 0-th period.

P^i_t : an n-dimensional row vector denoting the money prices of goods (excluding money and bonds) in the t-th period, as expected by the i-th household at the beginning of the 0-th period.

$P_{o,n+1}$: the bond price in the 0-th period.[13]

$P^i_{t,n+1}$: the bond price in the t-th period, as expected by the i-th household at the beginning of the 0-th period.

$\pi_{t,k}$: the k-th firm's profit in the t-th period which the firm divides among the rentiers.

$\pi^i_{t,k}$: the k-th firm's profit in the t-th period, as expected by the i-th rentier at the beginning of the 0-th period.

$\alpha^i_{t,k}$: the i-th rentier's share (ratio) in the k-th firm's (k=1,2, ..., μ) profit in the t-th period.

---

12. The money price of a bond in the t-th period is $P_{t,n+1}$. Since $\frac{1}{P_{t,n+1}} - 1$ = the interest rate, the amount of money per bond to be received in the t+1-th period includes both the principal and the interest.

13. Cf. footnote 12.

$\kappa^i_{t,j}$: The i-th household obtains cash by selling the j-th good including labour (j=1,2, ..., n) in the t-th period. The household can use this cash for purchases only after making the sale. The household expects to be able to use, in the t-th period, some part of the cash obtained by selling the j-th good. The ratio of this part to the cash obtained by selling the j-th good is denoted by $\kappa^i_{t,j}$. The remainder of the cash will be kept for the next week.[14]

$\kappa^i_{t,n+1}$: The i-th household obtains cash also by selling the n+1-th good, *i.e.*, a bond, as well. In other words, the household can obtain cash by borrowing money from other economic units. This cash can be used for purchases only after completing the transaction. Thus, the household expects to be able to use, in the t-th period, some part of the cash obtained by selling the bond. The ratio of this part to the cash obtained by selling the bond is denoted by $\kappa^i_{t,n+1}$. The remainder will be held for the following week.

$\kappa^i_{t,b}$: The i-th household which holds a bond in the t-th period can expect the receipt of the cash in the t+1-th period. For example, if the i-th household demands bonds (that is, $x^i_{t,n+1} > 0$) in the t-th period, this household expends a money sum worth $P_{o,n+1}x^i_{o,n+1}$ or $P^i_{t,n+1}x^i_{t,n+1}$ in the t-th period (t=1,2, ..., τ-1) and can expect to receive the cash worth of one dollar $\times\ x^i_{t,n+1}$ in the t+1-th period. That is, the cash, as the principal plus the interest, is repaid to the household. The household can use this cash for buying activity only after repayment of the bond. The household expects to be able to use in the t+1-th period some part of the cash obtained by repayment. The ratio of this part to the cash repaid is denoted by

---

14. Cf. Assumptions IV.2 and IV.3 on pp. 33-34.

$\kappa^i_{t,b}$.

D^i_t : a subset of an n-dimensional space. This subset denotes the i-th household's preference field in the t-th period ($t=0,1,2, \ldots, \tau$) of goods (excluding bonds and money).

1.2 The Labourer's Maximization Behaviour

Now, let the final period of planning time horizon be τ. Then the i-th labourer's utility function is[15]

$$\text{(1.i)} \qquad u^i(x^i_o, x^i_1, \ldots, x^i_\tau), \quad i=1,2, \ldots, h.$$

The labourer chooses $(x^i_t, x^i_{t,n+1}, x^i_{t,o})$, $t=0,1, \ldots, \tau$, which maximizes the function (1.i), subject to $x^i_t \in D^i_t$, the following budget constraints (2.i), money constraints (2.i.a), and the third set of constraints (2.i.b). The meaning of this third set of constraints will be made clear below. Since Assumption IV.1, Assumptions V.1,2,4, 5,6, and Assumption IX.1 exist, as will be given later, the budget constraints are as follows:

$$\text{(2.i)} \qquad \begin{aligned} & P_o x^i_o + P_{o,n+1} x^i_{o,n+1} + x^i_{o,o} \leqq \bar{x}^i_{o,o} + P_o \bar{x}^i_o \\ & P^i_1 x^i_1 + P^i_{1,n+1} x^i_{1,n+1} + x^i_{1,o} \leqq x^i_{o,n+1} + x^i_{o,o} \\ & \cdots\cdots\cdots\cdots\cdots\cdots\cdots\cdots\cdots\cdots \\ & P^i_\tau x^i_\tau \leqq x^i_{\tau-1,n+1} + x^i_{\tau-1,o} \\ & x^i_{t,1} \leqq 0, \quad t=0,1, \ldots, \tau; \\ & \qquad\qquad i=1,2, \ldots, h. \end{aligned}$$

From Assumption IV.2 which states the property of money, and Assumptions V.1,2, 4,5,6, together with the definitions of $\kappa^i_{t,j}$ ($j=1,2, \ldots, n+1$) and $\kappa^i_{t,b}$, the money

15. Actually, the final period of planning time horizon differs for each household. But, without loss of generality, we can assume that the final periods of all households and firms are the same and thus we will adopt the same notation τ.

constraints are as follows:[16]

$$\sum_{j=2}^{n}\max\{P_{o,j}(x^i_{o,j}-\bar{x}^i_{o,j}),0\}+\max(P_{o,n+1}x^i_{o,n+1},0)$$

$$\leqq \bar{x}^i_{o,o}-\kappa^i_{o,1}P_{o,1}x^i_{o,1}+\sum_{j=2}^{n}\max\{\kappa^i_{o,j}P_{o,j}(\bar{x}^i_{o,j}-x^i_{o,j}),0\}$$

$$+\max(-\kappa^i_{o,n+1}P_{o,n+1}x^i_{o,n+1},0)$$

(2.i.a)
$$\sum_{j=2}^{n}P^i_{1,j}x^i_{1,j}+\max(P^i_{1,n+1}x^i_{1,n+1},0)+\max(-x^i_{o,n+1},0)$$

$$\leqq x^i_{o,o}-\kappa^i_{1,1}P^i_{1,1}x^i_{1,1}+\max(\kappa^i_{o,b}x^i_{o,n+1},0)$$

$$+\max(-\kappa^i_{1,n+1}P^i_{1,n+1}x^i_{1,n+1},0)$$

....

$$\sum_{j=2}^{n}P^i_{\tau,j}x^i_{\tau,j}+\max(-x^i_{\tau-1,n+1},0)$$

$$\leqq x^i_{\tau-1,o}-\kappa^i_{\tau,1}P^i_{\tau,1}x^i_{\tau,1}+\max(\kappa^i_{\tau-1,b}x^i_{\tau-1,n+1},0),$$

$$i=1,2,\ \ldots,\ h.$$

The third set of constraints, which comes from Assumption V.3 and represents a relation between the demand for (or supply of) bonds in two successive periods, is as follows:

(2.i.b)
$$\underline{\Delta}\leqq x^i_{t,n+1}-x^i_{t+1,n+1}\leqq\Delta,\quad t=0,1,2,\ \ldots,\ \tau-1;$$

$$i=1,2,\ \ldots,\ h.$$

1.3 The Rentier's Maximization Behaviour

The rentier chooses $(x^i_t,\ x^i_{t,n+1},\ x^i_{t,o})$, $t=0,1,\ \ldots,\ \tau$, which maximizes the function (1.ii), subject to $x^i_t\in D^i_t$, the following budget constraints (2.ii), money constraints (2.ii.a), and the third set of constraints (2.ii.b).

---

16. The formulation $\max\{\kappa^i_{o,j}P_{o,j}(\bar{x}^i_{o,j}-x^i_{o,j}),0\}$ in the money constraints is also seen in Grandmont, J. and Younes, Y. [5]. Haga [8] has made this formulation independently of them. This formulation is concerned with the selling side, but, in Haga a similar formulation, *i.e.*, $\max\{\bar{\kappa}^i_{o,j}P_{o,j}(x^i_{o,j}-\underline{\bar{x}}^i_{o,j}),0\}$, was adopted on the buying side also. (The assignment of notations κ and $\bar{\kappa}$ were reversed there.) At

The rentier's utility function (1.ii) is

$$\text{(1.ii)} \qquad u^i(x^i_o,\ x^i_1,\ \ldots,\ x^i_\tau), \quad i=h+1,\ h+2,\ \ldots,\ \ell.$$

Since, in addition to the assumptions mentioned above in relation to the labourer's budget constraints (2.i), we impose Assumption IX.1 and Assumption IX.2, the rentier's budget constraints are as follows:

$$\text{(2.ii)} \qquad \begin{aligned}
&P_o x^i_o + P_{o,n+1} x^i_{o,n+1} + x^i_{o,o} \leqq \bar{x}^i_{o,o} + P_o \bar{x}^i_o + \sum_{k=1}^{\mu} \alpha^i_{o,k} \pi_{o,k} \\
&P^i_1 x^i_1 + P^i_{1,n+1} x^i_{1,n+1} + x^i_{1,o} \leqq x^i_{o,n+1} + x^i_{o,o} + \sum_{k=1}^{\mu} \alpha^i_{1,k} \pi_{1,k} \\
&\ldots\ldots\ldots\ldots\ldots\ldots\ldots\ldots\ldots\ldots\ldots\ldots \\
&P^i_\tau x^i_\tau \leqq x^i_{\tau-1,n+1} + x^i_{\tau-1,o} + \sum_{k=1}^{\mu} \alpha^i_{\tau,k} \pi_{\tau,k} \\
&x^i_{t,1} = 0, \quad t=0,1,\ \ldots,\ \tau; \\
&\qquad\qquad i=h+1,\ h+2,\ \ldots,\ \ell.
\end{aligned}$$

By Assumptions IV.5 and IX.1, the rentier's money constraints are not (2.i.a), but (2.ii.a); that is,

$$\text{(2.ii.a)} \qquad \begin{aligned}
&\sum_{j=2}^{n} \max\{P_{o,j}(x^i_{o,j} - \bar{x}^i_{o,j}),0\} + \max(P_{o,n+1} x^i_{o,n+1},0) \\
&\leqq \bar{x}^i_{o,o} + \sum_{j=2}^{n} \max\{\kappa^i_{o,j} P_{o,j}(\bar{x}^i_{o,j} - x^i_{o,j}),0\} \\
&+ \max(-\kappa^i_{o,n+1} P_{o,n+1} x^i_{o,n+1},0) \\
&\sum_{j=2}^{n} P^i_{1,j} x^i_{1,j} + \max(P^i_{1,n+1} x^i_{1,n+1},0) + \max(-x^i_{o,n+1},0) \\
&\leqq x^i_{o,o} + \max(\kappa^i_{o,b} x^i_{o,n+1},0) + \max(-\kappa^i_{1,n+1} P^i_{1,n+1} x^i_{1,n+1},0) \\
&\ldots\ldots\ldots\ldots\ldots\ldots\ldots\ldots\ldots\ldots\ldots\ldots \\
&\sum_{j=2}^{n} P^i_{\tau,j} x^i_{\tau,j} + \max(-x^i_{\tau-1,n+1},0) \\
&\leqq x^i_{\tau-1,o} + \max(\kappa^i_{\tau-1,b} x^i_{\tau-1,n+1},0), \\
&\qquad\qquad i=h+1,\ h+2,\ \ldots,\ \ell.
\end{aligned}$$

---

present we think this second formulation unnecessary.

The third set of constraints is, as in case of the labourer, as follows:

(2.ii.b) $\underline{\Delta} \leqq x^{i}_{t,n+1} - x^{i}_{t+1,n+1} \leqq \Delta$, $t=0,1,2, \ldots, \tau-1;$

$i=h+1, h+2, \ldots, \ell.$

2. The Firm

The third economic unit of our model is the firm. (The other economic units are the labourer household and the rentier household.)

2.1 Notation

The number of firms is μ.

y^{k}_{t} : an n-dimensional column vector which denotes the k-th firm's net input or net output in the t-th period.

$y^{k}_{t,j}$: the j-th element of y^{k}_{t}, namely, the net input (in the case where $y^{k}_{t,j} < 0$) or the net output (in the case where $y^{k}_{t,j} \geqq 0$) of the j-th good. $y^{k}_{t,1}$ represents the net input of labour in the t-th period.

$\bar{y}^{k}_{o}$: an n-dimensional column vector which denotes the k-th firm's initial holdings of goods in the 0-th period.

$y^{k}_{t,n+1}$: a scalar which denotes the k-th firm's net demand (in the case where $y^{k}_{t,n+1} \geqq 0$) or net supply (in the case where $y^{k}_{t,n+1} < 0$) of bonds. The meaning of the notation $y^{k}_{t,n+1}$ will become clearer if one refers to $x^{i}_{t,n+1}$ on pp. 6-7 above.

$y^{k}_{t,o}$: the k-th firm's *ex ante* demand for money stock at the end of the t-th period.

$\bar{y}^{k}_{o,o}$: the k-th firm's initial holding of money stock at the beginning of the 0-th period.

$\bar{y}^{k}_{o,j}$: $\bar{y}^{k}_{o,j}$ is the j-th element of the vector $\bar{y}^{k}_{o}$ which denotes the k-th firm's initial holding of the j-th good, excluding bonds and money stock: $j=2,3, \ldots, n; j \neq 1, j \neq n+1$.

p^k_t : an n-dimensional row vector denoting the money prices of goods (excluding bonds and money) in the t-th period, as expected by the k-th firm at the beginning of the 0-th period.

$p^k_{t,n+1}$: the money price of bonds in the t-th period, as expected by the k-th firm at the beginning of the 0-th period.

$\kappa^k_{t,j}$: The k-th firm expects to be able to use in the t-th period some part of the cash obtained by selling the j-th good ($j=1,2, \ldots, n$) actually produced in the same period. The ratio of this part to the cash obtained is denoted by $\kappa^k_{t,j}$. The meaning of the notation $\kappa^k_{t,j}$ will become clearer if one refers to $\kappa^i_{t,j}$ on p.8 above.

$\kappa^k_{t,n+1}$: The k-th firm also expects to be able to use, in the t-th period, some part of the cash obtained by selling the n+1-th good, *i.e.*, a bond. The ratio of this part to the cash obtained by borrowing is denoted by $\kappa^k_{t,n+1}$. The meaning of the notation $\kappa^k_{t,n+1}$ will become clearer if one refers to $\kappa^i_{t,n+1}$ on p.8 above.

$\bar{\kappa}^k_{t,j}$: The k-th firm expects to be able to use in the t-th period some part of the cash obtained by selling the j-th good in stock (excluding labour and bonds) already existing at the beginning of the t-th period. The ratio of this part to the cash obtained by selling the j-th good in stock, is denoted by $\bar{\kappa}^k_{t,j}$.

$\kappa^k_{t,b}$: The k-th firm which holds a bond in the t-th period can expect to receive, in the t+1-th period, the cash worth of the principal plus interest. The firm can use this cash for buying activity only after receipt of the principal plus interest. The firm expects to be able to use, in the t+1-th period, some part of this cash received. The ratio of this part to the cash received is denoted by $\kappa^k_{t,b}$.

The meaning of the notation $\kappa^{k}_{t,b}$ will become clearer if one refers to $\kappa^{i}_{t,b}$ on pp. 8-9 above.

β^k : β^k is the cash balance remaining at the end of the τ-th period other than the cash which corresponds to the profit. In the case of either $y^k_{\tau-1,n+1} \geqq 0$ or $y^k_{\tau-1,n+1} < 0$, β^k is actually equal to the sum of $(y^k_{\tau-1,n+1} + y^k_{\tau-1,o})$, as will be explained below. Moreover, from Assumption VI.1 given below, when β^k is positive, it must be divided among the rentiers as a part of their shares, together with the (gross) profit. On the other hand, when β^k is negative, the amount $|\beta^k|$ must be subtracted from the gross profit before the profit is divided among the rentiers.

$\pi_{o,k}$: the k-th firm's profit in the 0-th period. (See $\pi_{t,k}$ on p.7).

$\pi^k_{t,k}$: the k-th firm's profit in the t-th period, as expected by the k-th firm at beginning of the 0-th period.

$\Pi_{o,k}$: the present value of the k-th firm's future flow of profits (t=0,1, ..., τ) calculated at the beginning of the 0-th period.

Q^k_t : the k-th firm's production set in the t-th period, that is, the set of all feasible production vectors y^k_t.

2.2 The Firm's Maximization Behaviour

The k-th firm chooses $(y^k_t, y^k_{t,n+1}, y^k_{t,o})$, t=0,1,2, ..., τ,[17] which maximizes its present value $\Pi_{o,k}$ defined in (1.iii), subject to $y^k_t \in Q^k_t$, the budget constraints

---

17. Note that the values of $y^k_{\tau,n+1}$ and $y^k_{\tau,o}$ are both zero.

(3), the money constraints (3.a), and two more sets of constraints (3.b) and (3.c). The last set of constraints (3.c) will be clarified below.

Now, by definition, $\pi_{o,k} = P_o y_o^k$, $\pi_{1,k}^k = P_1^k y_1^k$, ..., $\pi_{\tau-1,k}^k = P_{\tau-1}^k y_{\tau-1}^k$, and then by the definition of β^k,

$$\pi_{\tau,k}^k = P_\tau^k y_\tau^k + \beta^k, \qquad k=1,2, \ldots, \mu.$$

Thus the k-firm's present value is

$$\begin{aligned} \Pi_{o,k} &= P_o y_o^k + P_{o,n+1} P_1^k y_1^k + P_{o,n+1} P_{1,n+1}^k P_2^k y_2^k \\ &+ \ldots\ldots\ldots\ldots + P_{o,n+1} P_{1,n+1}^k P_{2,n+1}^k \times \ldots \\ &\times P_{\tau-1,n+1}^k (P_\tau^k y_\tau^k + \beta^k), \\ &\qquad\qquad k=1,2, \ldots, \mu. \end{aligned} \tag{1.iii}$$

From Assumption IV.1 and Assumptions V.1,2,4,5,6, the k-th firm's budget constraints are as follows:

$$\sum_{j=1}^{n} \max(-P_{o,j} y_{o,j}^k, 0) + P_{o,n+1} y_{o,n+1}^k + y_{o,o}^k$$
$$\leqq \bar{y}_{o,o}^k + P_o \bar{y}_o^k + \sum_{j=1}^{n} \max(P_o y_{o,j}^k, 0) - \pi_{o,k}$$

$$\begin{aligned} &\sum_{j=1}^{n} \max(-P_{1,j}^k y_{1,j}^k, 0) + P_{1,n+1}^k y_{o,n+1}^k + y_{1,o}^k \\ &\leqq y_{o,o}^k + y_{o,n+1}^k + \sum_{j=1}^{n} \max(P_{1,j}^k y_{1,j}^k, 0) - \pi_{1,k}^k \\ &\ldots\ldots\ldots\ldots\ldots\ldots\ldots\ldots\ldots\ldots\ldots\ldots \\ &\sum_{j=1}^{n} \max(-P_{\tau,j}^k y_{\tau,j}^k, 0) \leqq y_{\tau-1,o}^k + y_{\tau-1,n+1}^k \\ &\qquad + \sum_{j=1}^{n} \max(P_{\tau,j}^k y_{\tau,j}^k, 0) - \pi_{\tau,k}^k, \\ &\qquad k=1,2, \ldots, \mu. \end{aligned} \tag{3}$$

Here, let us define I^k and $\tilde{I}^k$ as follows:[18]

---

18. In other words, I^k is a set which consists of subscript j of the k-th

$$I^k=\{j \mid y^k_{o,j} \geqq 0, \quad j=2,3, \ldots, n\}$$

$$\tilde{I}^k=\{j \mid y^k_{o,j} < 0, \quad j=1,2, \ldots, n\}$$

From Assumptions IV.2,and VI.1, the k-th firm's money constraints are as follows:[19]

(3.a)

$$\sum_{j=1}^{n}\max\{-P_{o,j}(y^k_{o,j}+\bar{y}^k_{o,j}),0\}+\max(P_{o,n+1}y^k_{o,n+1},0)$$

$$\leqq \bar{y}_{o,o}+\sum_{j\in I^k}P_{o,j}(\bar{\kappa}^k_{o,j}\bar{y}^k_{o,j}+\kappa^k_{o,j}y^k_{o,j})$$

$$+\sum_{j\in\tilde{I}^k}\max\{\kappa^k_{o,j}P_{o,j}(\bar{y}^k_{o,j}+y^k_{o,j}),0\}+\max(-\kappa^k_{o,n+1}P_{o,n+1}y^k_{o,n+1},0)$$

$$\sum_{j=1}^{n}\max(-P^k_{1,j}y^k_{1,j},0)+\max(P^k_{1,n+1}y^k_{1,n+1},0)$$

$$+\max(-y^k_{o,n+1},0)\leqq y^k_{o,o}+\sum_{j=1}^{n}\max(\kappa^k_{1,j}P^k_{1,j}y^k_{1,j},0)$$

$$+\max(\kappa^k_{o,b}y^k_{o,n+1},0)+\max(-\kappa^k_{1,n+1}P^k_{1,n+1}y^k_{1,n+1},0)$$

$$\cdots\cdots\cdots\cdots\cdots\cdots\cdots\cdots\cdots\cdots\cdots\cdots$$

$$\sum_{j=1}^{n}\max(-P^k_{\tau,j}y^k_{\tau,j},0)+\max(-y^k_{\tau-1,n+1},0)$$

$$\leqq y^k_{\tau-1,o}+\sum_{j=1}^{n}\max(\kappa^k_{\tau,j}P^k_{\tau,j}y^k_{\tau,j},0)$$

$$+\max(\kappa^k_{\tau-1,b}y^k_{\tau-1,n+1},0),$$

$$k=1,2,\ldots,\mu.$$

This set of inequalities is the k-th firm's money constraints.[20]

---

firm's net output in the 0-th period (*i.e.*, $y^k_{o,j} \geqq 0$). $\tilde{I}^k$ is a set which consists of subscript j of the k-th firm's net input in the 0-th period (*i.e.*, $y^k_{o,j} < 0$).

19. In Haga [8], we adopted the input in the form of money, following Walras [24], instead of the formulation (3.a) described below. The input in the form of money itself corresponds to that part of the real input which the firm must buy when needed and for which it therefore must hold cash balances. Walras's input in the form of money is of this sort. It is due to the suggestion of a graduate student, Mr. R. Okumura, that we were able to formulate it as (3). However, formulation (3) is actually equivalent to that in Haga [8]. (Cf. Walras [24] pp. 315-324.)

20. As for the second term in the right-hand side of the first inequality in (3.a), at first we tried to formulate it as $\sum_{j=1}^{n}\max\{\kappa^k_{o,j}P_{o,j}(\bar{y}^k_{o,j}+y^k_{o,j}),0\}$, but we

The third set of constraints, as in the case of the household, is as follows:

(3.b) $\quad \underline{\Delta} \leqq y^k_{t,n+1} - y^k_{t+1,n+1} \leqq \Delta, \qquad t=0,1,2, \ldots, \tau-1; \quad k=1,2, \ldots, \mu.$

The fourth set of constraints which comes from Assumption IX.3, given below, implies that any planned labour input level is limited in every period $t(t\neq 0)$. This set of constraints is:

(3.c) $\quad \bar{b}_t \leqq y^k_{t,1}, \qquad t=1,2, \ldots, \tau; \quad k=1,2, \ldots, \mu.$

The fifth constraint which comes from Assumption VI.2 is:

(3.d) $\quad \pi^k_{\tau,k} = P^k_\tau y^k_\tau + \beta^k \geqq 0.$

In fact, the fifth set of constraints which comes directly from Assumption VI.2 is that $\pi_{o,k} \geqq 0$, $\pi^k_{t,k} \geqq 0$ $(t=1,2, \ldots, \tau-1)$ and $\pi^k_{\tau,k} = P^k_\tau y^k_\tau + \beta^k \geqq 0$. But, as will be shown later, $\pi_{o,k}$ and $\pi^k_{t,k}$ $(t=1,2, \ldots, \tau-1)$ are non-negative in the firm's subjective equilibrium. Accordingly, we can drop the inequalities $\pi_{o,k} \geqq 0$ and $\pi^k_{t,k} \geqq 0$ $(t=1,2, \ldots, \tau-1)$ from the fifth set of constraints. On the other hand, even in the firm's subjective equilibrium, the sign of $\pi^k_{\tau,k}$ is indeterminate, although $P^k_\tau y^k_\tau$ is non-negative. Thus, only the inequality $\pi^k_{\tau,k} = P^k_\tau y^k_\tau + \beta^k \geqq 0$ remains.

Note that the profit in the t-th period $(t=0,1, \ldots, \tau)$, must be discounted in calculating the present value (1.iii). As defined on p.15, the profit, except in

---

finally adopted $\sum_{j\in I^k} P_{o,j}(\bar{\kappa}^k_{o,j}\bar{y}^k_{o,j} + \kappa^k_{o,j}y^k_{o,j})$. This is because the value of $\bar{\kappa}^k_{o,j}$, corresponding to <u>goods in stock</u> already existing at the beginning of the period, is very different from the value of $\kappa^k_{o,j}$ corresponding to the net outputs which emerge toward the end of the period due to "output lag". On the other hand, we adopted $\sum_{j\in \tilde{I}^k} \max\{\kappa^k_{o,j} P_{o,j}(\bar{y}^k_{o,j} + y^k_{o,j}), 0\}$ as the formulation in the third term, because in the case of net inputs, we need not consider "output lag".

the τ-th period, is $p_o y_o^k$, $p_1^k y_1^k$, ..., $p_{\tau-1}^k y_{\tau-1}^k$. But usually, if the firm sells a bond for the sake of its own activity, it subtracts the interest charge in the corresponding period from the profit, and after that, divides the <u>net</u> profit among the rentiers. Hence, in the usual calculation of the present value, the firm discounts the future flow of <u>net</u> profit, which is the profit minus interest charge.

We did not adopt the usual calculation because the firm which supplied the bond (or borrowed money) will be able to continue to supply bonds to repay the principal plus interest, and moreover to carry forward its own debt until the final period τ, when it will clear all accounts at the same time. Therefore, the net profit to be divided among the rentiers in the τ-th period is $p_\tau^k y_\tau^k + \beta^k$.[21] Although our method seems different from the usual, we think that ultimately both are the same, because the firm's debt or credit (including the principal plus interest), which has been carried forward, is cleared off all at the same time, being subtracted from the profit in the τ-th period.[22]

---

21. When a set of inequalities (3)' is given below, we will show that β^k is equal to $y_{\tau-1,n+1}^k + y_{\tau-1,o}^k$.

22. Solow says that the current cost of the circulating capital does not bring about the interest charge. (See Solow [23] pp. 32-34.) The reader may refer to Solow, though his idea differs somewhat from ours.

CHAPTER III

THE GENERAL EQUILIBRIUM SYSTEM UNDER THE "DUAL-DECISION HYPOTHESIS"

——Disequilibrium-Equilibrium Model——

Let us begin by first explaining the standard equilibrium model. Then we will explain the equilibrium model under the dual-decision hypothesis. Finally we will explain the assumptions of our model.

1. The Standard General Market Equilibrium and the General Market Equilibrium under the "Dual-Decision Hypothesis"

1.1 Notation

$\bar{Z}_o$: The entire society's initial holding of money stock at the beginning of the 0-th period, *i.e.*,

$$\bar{Z}_o = \sum_{i=1}^{\ell} \bar{x}^i_{o,o} + \sum_{k=1}^{\mu} \bar{y}^k_{o,o}.$$

1.2 The Standard General Market Equilibrium Condition

Let $(\hat{x}^i_o, \hat{x}^i_{o,n+1}, \hat{x}^i_{o,o})$ and $(\hat{y}^k_o, \hat{y}^k_{o,n+1}, \hat{y}^k_{o,o})$ denote the vectors in the 0-th period of goods, bonds and money which result from the maximization behaviour of the i-th household and the k-th firm respectively. Then, the standard market equilibrium system, not considering futures markets is as follows:

$$\begin{aligned} &\sum_{i=1}^{\ell} \hat{x}^i_o = \sum_{k=1}^{\mu} \hat{y}^k_o + \sum_{i=1}^{\ell} \bar{x}^i_o + \sum_{k=1}^{\mu} \bar{y}^k_o \\ (4) \qquad &\sum_{i=1}^{\ell} \hat{x}^i_{o,n+1} + \sum_{k=1}^{\mu} \hat{y}^k_{o,n+1} = 0 \\ &\sum_{i=1}^{\ell} \hat{x}^i_{o,o} + \sum_{k=1}^{\mu} \hat{y}^k_{o,o} = \bar{Z}_o. \end{aligned}$$

These equations represent the equilibria of goods (including labour, bond, and money) markets. These equilibria are the usual and orthodox equilibria in the sense that the *ex ante* demands for goods are equal to the respective *ex ante* supplies. Of course, this is also true for the equilibrium of the labour market.

1.3 The General Market Equilibrium Condition under the "Dual-Decision Hypothesis"

Our model is a special equilibrium model in that it combines elements of both Walras and Keynes, using Glustoff's re-interpretation of Keynes. We adopt the dual-decision hypothesis, to be precisely formulated below, under which the labourer, looking at the existence of an excess supply in the labour market, will alter his plan about the quantity of labour to supply. At the same time he will alter his plan about his demand for other goods, including bonds and money.

Let $(\tilde{x}_o^i, \tilde{x}_{o,n+1}^i, \tilde{x}_{o,o}^i)$ denote the vector in the 0-th period of goods, bonds, and money which the labourer demands after the dual-decision. The new equilibrium market conditions are as follows:

$$
(5)\qquad
\begin{aligned}
&\sum_{i=1}^{h}\tilde{x}_o^i + \sum_{i=h+1}^{\ell}\hat{x}_o^i = \sum_{k=1}^{\mu}\hat{y}_o^k + \sum_{i=1}^{\ell}\bar{x}_o^i + \sum_{k=1}^{\mu}\bar{y}_o^k \\
&\sum_{i=1}^{h}\tilde{x}_{o,n+1} + \sum_{i=h+1}^{\ell}\hat{x}_{o,n+1}^i + \sum_{k=1}^{\mu}\hat{y}_{o,n+1}^k = 0 \\
&\sum_{i=1}^{h}\tilde{x}_{o,o}^i + \sum_{i=h+1}^{\ell}\hat{x}_{o,o}^i + \sum_{k=1}^{\mu}\hat{y}_o^k = \bar{Z}_o .
\end{aligned}
$$

The first equation of (5) represents the labour and product market equilibria. The second represents the bond market equilibrium. The third represents the money market equilibrium. Our new labour market equilibrium does not deny the existence of excess supply in the usual and orthodox sense, and for this reason, our labour market may be said to be in disequilibrium. However, it requires that the supply of labour decided upon by the dual-decision process be equal to the demand for labour. Accordingly, our labour market equilibrium condition must be a strict equality.

2. Assumptions of the Model

Now, the assumptions of our model are as follows.

Assumption I.1 : Let vector b_t^i denote the infimum of D_t^i. Then $D_t^i = b_t^i$

$+ R^n_+$.[23] The first element of b^i_t, which corresponds to labour, is negative and the other elements of b^i_t are zero. Thus D^i_t is a closed and convex set, $i=1,2, \ldots, \ell$; $t=1,2, \ldots, \tau$.

I.2 : $\bar{x}^i_{o,1} = 0$, $i=1,2, \ldots, \ell$, and $\bar{y}^k_{o,1} = 0$, $k=1,2, \ldots, \mu$. This assumption $\bar{x}^i_{o,1} = 0$ relates to the assumption in I.1 that the infimum of labour demand is negative. $\bar{y}^k_{o,1} = 0$ indicates that the firm does not own any labour.

I.3 : $u^i(x^i_o, x^i_1, \ldots, x^i_\tau)$ is a single-valued continuous function of $(x^i_o, x^i_1, \ldots, x^i_\tau)$.

I.4 : For every household i, $u^i(x^i_o, x^i_1, \ldots, x^i_\tau)$ is a strictly concave function. That is, if $u^i(x^i_o, x^i_1, \ldots, x^i_\tau) \geqq \omega$ and $u^i(x^{i^\alpha}_o, x^{i^\alpha}_1, \ldots, x^{i^\alpha}_\tau) \geqq \omega$, then $u(\lambda x^i_o + (1-\lambda)x^{i^\alpha}_o, \lambda x^i_1 + (1-\lambda)x^{i^\alpha}_1, \ldots, \lambda x^i_\tau + (1-\lambda)x^{i^\alpha}_\tau) > \omega$, for every real number ω, and $0 < \lambda < 1$.

I.5 : For every household i, $u^i(x^i_o, x^i_1, \ldots, x^i_\tau)$ is a strictly monotone increasing function of $(x^i_o, x^i_1, \ldots, x^i_\tau)$.[24]

---

23. D^i_t is the set $D^i_t = \{x^i_t \mid x^i_t = b^i_t + x^i_t ; \; x^i_t \in R^n_+\}$.

24. $(x^i_o, x^i_1, \ldots, x^i_\tau)$ can be called neither a row vector nor a column vector, as x^i_t $(t=0,1, \ldots, \tau)$ is a column vector. However, it is clear that it is still an $n(\tau+1)$-dimensional vector, because linear operations on vectors can be performed in $R^{n(\tau+1)}$. The order relation of this vector $(x^i_o, x^i_1, \ldots, x^i_\tau)$ is defined in the

Assumption II.1 : For every household i, $\bar{x}^i_{o,j} > 0$ for at least one j (j=0,2, ..., n; $j\neq 1$).[25] That is, every household has positive initial holdings of at least one good. Moreover, $\sum_{i=h+1}^{\ell} \bar{x}^i_{o,j} > 0$ for j (j=0,2, ..., n; $j\neq 1$). That is, an initial stock (in the 0-th period) of every good, including money stock, is held by at least one rentier.

II.2 : If the i-th rentier expects the prices of all goods, $p^i_{t,j}$ (t=1,2, ..., τ; j=1,2, ..., n; i=h+1,h+2, ..., ℓ) to be positive, then he will expect to receive some positive dividend in at least one period during the periods from 1 to τ-1.[26] That is, $\sum_{k=1}^{\mu} \alpha^i_{t,k} \pi^i_{t,k}$ is positive for at least one t ($t\neq\tau$), where $\alpha^i_{t,k} \geqq 0$ (t=0,1, ..., τ; k=1,2, ..., μ) and $\sum_{k=1}^{\mu} \alpha^i_{t,k} > 0$ (t=0,1, ..., τ).

---

following way: an inequality sign between vectors $(x_o^{i^\alpha}, x_1^{i^\alpha}, \ldots, x_\tau^{i^\alpha}) \geq (x_o^{i^\beta}, x_1^{i^\beta}, \ldots, x_\tau^{i^\beta})$ is the same as an inequality between column vectors $(x_o^{i^{\alpha'}}, x_1^{i^{\alpha'}}, \ldots, x_\tau^{i^{\alpha'}})' \geq (x_o^{i^{\beta'}}, x_1^{i^{\beta'}}, \ldots, x_\tau^{i^{\beta'}})'$ or as an inequality sign between row vectors $(x_o^{i^{\alpha'}}, x_1^{i^{\alpha'}}, \ldots, x_\tau^{i^{\alpha'}}) \geq (x_o^{i^{\beta'}}, x_1^{i^{\beta'}}, \ldots, x_\tau^{i^{\beta'}})$, where the prime ' represents the transpose of each vector. For example, for column vectors x and y, $x \geq y$ means that $x \geqq y$ but $x\neq y$. Readers who are accustomed to using row vectors or column vectors may interpret vector $(x^i_o, x^i_1, \ldots, x^i_\tau)$ as a column vector $(x_o^{i'}, x_1^{i'}, \ldots, x_\tau^{i'})'$ or as a row vector $(x_o^{i'}, x_1^{i'}, \ldots, x_\tau^{i'})$.

25. Notice that $j\neq 1$ and cf. Assumption I.2 given above.

26. This assumption does not require that the dividend in the τ-th period be positive. Of course the dividend in the τ-th period may be positive, although this positivity is <u>not necessary</u> for our existence proof. The reason why we impose Assumption II.2 is that we may be unable to ensure the lower semi-continuity of the mapping if the dividend is positive only in the τ-th period, as will be shown below. This lower semi-continuity is a necessary condition for the continuity of the mapping. The property of continuity is very important for our existence proof.

II.3 : For every firm, $\bar{y}^k_{o,j} > 0$ for at least one j (j=2, ..., n; j≠1). That is, every firm has positive initial holdings of at least one good.[27]

II.4 : $\bar{Z}_o$ is positive and the money stock of the whole society is constant throughout all the periods. ($\bar{Z}_o \geqq 1$.)

Assumption III.1 : For every k and t, Q^k_t is a convex and closed set which contains the zero vector.

III.2 : For any y^k_t, $y^{k^\alpha}_t$, and λ such that $y^k_t \in Q^k_t$, $y^{k^\alpha}_t \in Q^k_t$, and $0 < \lambda < 1$, there always exists a $y^{k^\beta}_t$ such that $y^{k^\beta}_t \in Q^k_t$ and $y^{k^\beta}_t \geqq \lambda y^k_t + (1-\lambda) y^{k^\alpha}_t$,[28] where y^k_t and $y^{k^\alpha}_t$ are different vectors, t=0,1,2, ..., τ; k=1,2, ..., μ.[29]

III.3 : For every t, $Q_t \cap (-Q_t) = \{0\}$, where $Q_t = \sum_{k=1}^{\mu} Q^k_t$, and {0} is the set consisting of the zero vector.

III.4 : The production process which produces a positive net output of at least one good requires a non-zero net input of the primary factor, labour. Thus for every t,

$Q^k_t \cap R^n_+ = \{0\}$.

III.5 : If the money wage is too high relative to all other prices and the money stock, then the firm cannot obtain non-negative profits by production processes other than the zero vector. We let $\hat{w}$ denote the level of the money wage above which such non-negative profits are impossible.

---

27. Of course, the firm's initial money stock $\bar{y}^k_{o,o}$ may be positive, although Assumption II.3 does not require it. Again, notice that j≠1 and cf. Assumption I.2.

28. Cf. footnote 24, concerning an inequality sign between vectors.

29. When this assumption is combined with convexity, Q^k_t is strictly convex. Cf. Intriligator [11] p. 461.

Assumption IV.1 : All contracts to buy and sell goods (including labour) and bonds are made only at the beginning of the week, namely, only on "Monday". On the other hand, the actual delivery and receipt of goods and bonds are made within the week. The payment and receipt of money are made within the week, also.

IV.2 : An economic unit can buy goods (including labour) and bonds from other economic units only with money. In other words, money is the general and sole means of exchange. The economic unit pays money when it purchases goods and bonds.

IV.3 : The values of $\kappa^i_{t,j}, \kappa^k_{t,j}, \bar{\kappa}^{k}_{t,j}, \kappa^i_{t,b}$, and $\kappa^k_{t,b}$ $(t=0,1, \ldots, \tau;$ $i=1,2, \ldots, \ell;$ $k=1,2, \ldots, \mu)$, as well as the values of $\kappa^i_{t,n+1}$ and $\kappa^k_{t,n+1}$ $(t=0,1, \ldots, \tau-1)$, are known by each economic unit, and they are constant.

Let us make some remarks concerning Assumption IV.2 and IV.3.

a) The demand for money stock arises from the property of money as the general and sole means of exchange. First, the receipt and payment of money during the period (or week) will not usually be synchronized, that is, there will usually be a discrepancy between the inflow and outflow of money. This discrepancy calls forth the demand for money stock. Second, an economic unit might find it more advantageous to postpone the purchase of goods or bonds until the following period. This will also call forth the demand for money stock.

b) The values of $\kappa^i_{t,j}, \kappa^k_{t,j}, \bar{\kappa}^{k}_{t,j}, \kappa^i_{t,b}$, and $\kappa^k_{t,b}$ $(t=0,1, \ldots, \tau;$ $i=1,2, \ldots, \ell;$ $k=1,2, \ldots, \mu)$, as well as the values of $\kappa^i_{t,n+1}$ and $\kappa^k_{t,n+1}$ $(t=0,1, \ldots, \tau-1)$ depend upon the extent to which the receipt and payment of money within each period are not synchronized. On the other hand, the larger the values of $\kappa^i_{t,j}, \kappa^k_{t,j}, \bar{\kappa}^{k}_{t,j}$ *etc.*, are, the smaller the economic unit's demand for money stock can generally be.[30]

IV.4 : For every household i and every firm k,

a) $0 \leqq \kappa^i_{t,j} \leqq 1,\ 0 \leqq \kappa^k_{t,j} \leqq 1,\ 0 \leqq \bar{\kappa}^k_{t,j} \leqq 1,$

$t=0,1,\ \ldots,\ \tau;\ j=1,2,\ \ldots,\ n.$

b) $0 \leqq \kappa^i_{t,b} \leqq 1,\ 0 \leqq \kappa^k_{t,b} \leqq 1,\quad t=0,1,\ \ldots,\ \tau-1.$

c) $0 \leqq \kappa^i_{t,n+1} < 1,\ 0 \leqq \kappa^k_{t,n+1} < 1,\quad t=0,1,\ \ldots,\ \tau-1.$[31]

IV.5 : The dividend is paid to the rentiers at the end of each period. Therefore, the rentiers cannot use the cash obtained as the dividend of each period for buying goods in the same period.

IV.6 : $0 < \kappa^i_{o,q} \leqq 1$ for every q-th good which the i-th household holds at the beginning of the 0-th period, $i=1,2,\ \ldots,\ \ell$.

$0 < \kappa^k_{o,q} \leqq 1$ and $0 < \bar{\kappa}^k_{o,q} \leqq 1$ for every q-th good which the k-th firm holds as initial holding at the beginning of the 0-th period, $k=1,2,\ \ldots,\ \mu$.[32]

IV.7 : There exists at least one firm k such that $\kappa^k_{o,j} = 0$,[33] $0 < \bar{\kappa}^k_{o,j} < 1$ for every $j \in I^k$ and $0 < \kappa^k_{o,j} < 1$ for every $j \in \tilde{I}^k$.[34]

---

30. Cf. the notation of $\kappa^i_{t,j}, \kappa^k_{t,j}, \kappa^i_{t,n+1}, \kappa^k_{t,n+1}, \kappa^i_{t,b}, \kappa^k_{t,b}$ *etc.* on pp. 8-9 and pp. 13-14.

31. The values of $\kappa^i_{t,j}, \kappa^k_{t,j}, \bar{\kappa}^k_{t,j}$ *etc.* are usually smaller than one, as are $\kappa^i_{t,n+1}$ and $\kappa^k_{t,n+1}$. But, what are decisively effective for our proof are the cases where $\kappa^i_{t,n+1} < 1$, $\kappa^k_{t,n+1} < 1$, and the strict inequalities in Assumption IV.6.

32. The q may be different for each household and firm.

33. This means that due to the "output lag", the output appears near the end of the period, and consequently, the cash revenue from the sale of this output cannot be used for buying goods within the same period.

34. Cf. pp. 15-16 concerning the notation of I^k and $\tilde{I}^k$.

IV.8 : For every firm, $\min_{j \in \tilde{I}^k} \kappa^k_{o,j} \geqq \max_{j \in I^k} \kappa^k_{o,j}$.

This means that each firm k can sell excess inventory of inputs, $\bar{y}^k_{o,j} + y^k_{o,j}$ (where $j \in \tilde{I}^k$),[35] whenever it wishes, even at the beginning of the 0-th period. However, all outputs will necessarily have a greater or lesser degree of output lag and hence, excess inventory of inputs is generally sold before current output.

IV.9 : For at least one rentier, $0 < \kappa^i_{t,n+1} < 1$, $t=0,1, \ldots, \tau-1$.[36]

IV.10: For at least one rentier, who has some real good other than money stock and bonds as his initial holding, $\kappa^i_{t,b} = 1$, $t=0,1, \ldots, \tau-1$.[37]

Assumption V.1 : $x^i_{\tau,o} = 0$ and $y^k_{\tau,o} = 0$, $i=1,2, \ldots, \ell$; $k=1,2, \ldots, \mu$.

That is, in the last period of the planning time horizon, no household nor firm demands any money stock.

V.2 : No household nor firm holds any bonds at the beginning of the 0-th period. That is, debt and credit from before the 0-th period have already been cleared by the beginning of the 0-th period.[38]

---

35. We may call $\bar{y}^k_{o,j} + y^k_{o,j}$, which is positive, excess inventory.

36. But it is not necessary that for every t ($t=0,1, \ldots, \tau-1$), $\kappa^i_{t,n+1}$ is positive. That is, if the expected dividend is positive in a period, say the $\tilde{t}$-th period (cf. Assumption II.2), it is not necessary that $\kappa^i_{t,n+1}$ ($t=\tilde{t}+1, \tilde{t}+2, \ldots, \tau-1$) after the $\tilde{t}$-th period should be positive.

37. This assumption means that if such a rentier demands a bond in the t-th period, then he expects to be able to receive, at the beginning of the t+1-th period, the cash worth of the principal plus interest. Cf. $\kappa^i_{t,b}$ on pp. 8-9.

38. As suggested in Negishi [16] pp. 34-35, this can be replaced by another, weaker, assumption. Particularly, see the end of column one, Negishi p. 35. However, if we use the weaker assumption, careful treatment would be required in the last stage of our proof. Cf. lines 8-10 of p. 96 below.

V.3 : For every household i and firm k, $\underline{\Delta} \leqq x^i_{t,n+1} - x^i_{t+1,n+1} \leqq \Delta$, and $\underline{\Delta} \leqq y^k_{t,n+1} - y^k_{t+1,n+1} \leqq \Delta$, $t=0,1, \ldots, \tau-2$, for a sufficiently large real number Δ and a sufficiently small real number $\underline{\Delta}$ such that $\Delta < \infty$ and $\underline{\Delta} > -\infty$. That is, each period's demand or supply from the household and the firm itself can be infinitely large (∞ or $-\infty$),[39] but the increment of demand or supply between two successive periods is not infinite.[40]

V.4 : The bond reaches maturity in one period and it is settled in the next period.

V.5 : For every household i and firm k, $x^i_{\tau,n+1} = 0$ and $y^k_{\tau,n+1} = 0$. That is, in the last period of the planning time horizon, no household nor firm demands any bonds.

V.6 : For every household i and firm k, $\bar{x}^i_{t,j} = 0$ and $\bar{y}^k_{t,j} = 0$, $t=1,2, \ldots, \tau$; $j=1,2, \ldots, n$. That is, every household and firm is endowed with a stock of goods only at the beginning of the 0-th period.

Of course, Assumption V.6 represents no more than a simplification of the problem, but we think this simplification is justified since Keynes himself does not explicitly take into consideration the existence of goods in future periods.[41]

---

39. Note that the net supply of bonds is represented by the negativity of $x^i_{t,n+1}$ and $y^k_{t,n+1}$. Also note that the demand and supply of bonds mean the <u>net</u> demand and <u>net</u> supply.

40. This assumption is important to ensure that the supply of bonds is bounded from below. This boundedness, in turn, plays a crucial role in our existence proof. It has often been asserted that the supply of bonds cannot be infinite, because there are limitations on the ability of economic units to redeem bonds. But, this assertion cannot directly be derived only from the usual constraints, *e.g.*, the budget constraints on the maximization behaviour of household and firm. For example, suppose that $x^i_{t,n+1}$ (or $y^k_{t,n+1}$) and $x^i_{t,o}$ (or $y^k_{t,o}$) can be $-\infty$ and ∞ respectively, when $P_{t,n+1}$ is equal to one. Such a case is not only mathematically possible, but also economically meaningful because our model contains the money constraints.

41. It is often assumed that, at the beginning of each period, stocks of

Assumption VI.1 : Every firm divides all the profits of the t-th period within the same period, immediately after it gains the profits.[42]

VI.2 : The k-th firm's profits (or expected profits) are gained from production except in the last period and hence

$$\pi_{o,k} = p_o y_o^k$$

and

$$\pi_{t,k}^k = p_t^k y_t^k, \quad t=1,2, \ldots, \tau-1.$$

In the last period, all remaining cash is divided among the rentiers and hence[43]

$$\pi_{\tau,k}^k = p_\tau^k y_\tau^k + \beta^k.$$

Also, $\pi_{o,k} \geqq 0$, $\pi_{t,k}^k \geqq 0$ where $k=1,2, \ldots, \mu$, $t=1,2, \ldots, \tau$. That is, all the firms adopt a dividend policy such that the dividend of each period should be non-negative.[44]

VI.3 : In the 0-th period, the dividend $\pi_{t,k}^i$ ($t=1,2, \ldots, \tau$; $k=1,2, \ldots, \mu$) is expected by the i-th rentier to be non-negative. The expected dividend $\pi_{t,k}^i$ depends on the prices

---

goods exist as endowments from heaven; but this is unwarranted in the present context, because our model, containing production, is different from a pure exchange economy. Therefore, we adopt Assumption V.6. Assumption V.6 is, however, rather awkward if the firm holds fixed capital goods. Thus we assume away the problem of fixed capital goods for the sake of simplicity.

42. In connection with Assumption IV.5, actually the firm gains the profits near the end of the period.

43. Cf. pp. 14-15 and pp. 17-18.

44. As will be shown later, $\pi_{o,k}$ and $\pi_{t,k}^k$ ($t=1,2, \ldots, \tau-1$; $t \neq \tau$) are non-negative in the firm's subjective equilibriumn, even without assuming their non-negativity. The reason why we give the non-negativity of $\pi_{o,k}$ and $\pi_{t,k}^k$ ($t=1,2, \ldots, \tau-1$; $t \neq \tau$) as an assumption is that we want to maintain consistency with Assumption VI.3. But even in the case of the maximum solution $\pi_{\tau,k}^k$ may be negative.

of goods (including labour and bonds) and on money stock in the 0-th period.[45] That is,

$$\pi^i_{t,k} = {}_t\pi^i_k(P_{o,1}, P_{o,2}, \ldots, P_{o,n+1}, \bar{x}^i_{o,o}),$$

$$t=1,2, \ldots, \tau.$$

${}_t\pi^i_k$ is a single-valued continuous function of

$(P_{o,1}, P_{o,2}, \ldots, P_{o,n+1}, \bar{x}^i_{o,o})$.

We need not assume that $\pi_{o,k} = {}_o\pi_k(P_{o,1}, P_{o,2}, \ldots, P_{o,n+1}, \bar{y}^k_{o,o})$ and $\pi^k_{t,k} = {}_t\pi^k_k(P_{o,1}, P_{o,2}, \ldots, P_{o,n+1}, \bar{y}^k_{o,o})$ are single valued and continuous, because below we will be able to offer proof that they are so, if $P_{o,j}$'s $(j=1,2, \ldots, n+1)$ are positive.

Assumption VII : There exists a minimum money wage, which is $\bar{w}$ in the 0-th period, below which the money wage cannot fall. This is attributable to social customs or government legislation.

a) This minimum money wage $\bar{w}$ depends on the prices of goods (excluding labour) and money stock in the 0-th period.[46] That is,

$$\bar{w} = w\,(P_{o,2}, P_{o,3}, \ldots, P_{o,n+1}, \bar{Z}_o)$$

and

$$\hat{w} > \bar{w}.$$

---

45. The reason why we regard money stock as a variable is that the real cash balance effect should be taken into account. That the rentier's expected dividend depends on his own money stock may cause some concern, but we think such treatment can be justified.

46. Keynes states that "It is sometimes said that it would be illogical for labour to resist a reduction of money-wages but not to resist a reduction of real wages. .... this might not be so illogical as it appears at first; and, as we shall see later, fortunately so. But, whether logical or illogical, experience shows that this is how labour in fact behaves." (Keynes [13] p. 9.) However, according to recent experience, the labourers resist a reduction of the real wage as well as a reduction of the money wage. Therefore, in general, the minimum money wage is determined by taking into account the prices of goods and other factors including money stock.

b) W is a single-valued continuous function of $(P_{o,2}, P_{o,3}, \ldots, P_{o,n+1}, \bar{Z}_o)$.

c) If all of these non-negative variables are not zero, then $\bar{w}$ is necessarily positive.[47]

d) This function is homogeneous of degree one with respect to these variables, excluding bond price.

Assumption VIII.1 : If the money wage in the 0-th period is positive, then,

a) the expected money wages $P^i_{t,1}$ and $P^k_{t,1}$ $(t=1,2, \ldots, \tau)$ are positive for any i and k,

b) the expected prices of goods $P^i_{t,j}$ and $P^k_{t,j}$ $(t=1,2, \ldots, \tau;\ j=2, \ldots, n)$ are positive for each i and k,[48] and

c) the expected bond prices $P^i_{t,n+1}$ and $P^k_{t,n+1}$ $(t=1,2, \ldots, \tau-1)$ are non-negative and not larger than one for any i and k.[49]

VIII.2 : If the bond price in the 0-th period $P_{o,n+1}$ is either positive or non-negative and smaller than one, then the expected bond prices $P^i_{t,n+1}$ and $P^k_{t,n+1}$ $(t=1,2, \ldots, \tau-1)$ are also respectively either positive or non-negative and smaller than one for any i and k.

---

47. It might seem strange that, even when only one of these variables (*e.g.* bond price) is positive, the minimum money wage is positive. But if we take into account the fact of Keynes' "downward rigidity" of the money wage, the positivity of the minimum wage in Assumption VII.c) will be plausible.

48. The plausibility of this assumption will be seen by referring to Assumption III.4.

49. The inequalities $P^i_{t,n+1} \leqq 1$ and $P^k_{t,n+1} \leqq 1$ imply that the interest rate is either zero or positive. Hence, in the normal case where a) and b) are satisfied, the plausibility of these inequalities will be clear. The plausibility of a non-negative bond price, which is the reciprocal of one plus the interest rate, will also be evident.

VIII.3 : The expected prices of goods (including labour and bonds) $P^i_{t,j}$ and $P^k_{t,j}$ ($t=1,2, \ldots, \tau$; $j=1,2, \ldots, n+1$) depend on the prices of goods (including labour and bonds) and money stock in the 0-th period. That is, for any i and k,

$$P^i_{t,j} = {}_tP^i_j(P_{o,1}, P_{o,2}, \ldots, P_{o,n+1}, \bar{x}^i_{o,o})$$

$$P^k_{t,j} = {}_tP^k_j(P_{o,1}, P_{o,2}, \ldots, P_{o,n+1}, \bar{y}^k_{o,o})$$

The functions ${}_tP^i_j$ and ${}_tP^k_j$ are single-valued and continuous.

VIII.4 : The functions ${}_tP^i_j$, ${}_tP^k_j$, and ${}_t\pi^i_k$ ($t=1,2, \ldots, \tau$; $j=1,2, \ldots, n$; $j \neq n+1$) are homogeneous of degree one with respect to the prices of goods (excluding bonds) and money stock in the 0-th period for any i and k. The functions ${}_tP^i_{n+1}$ and ${}_tP^k_{n+1}$ are homogeneous of degree zero with respect to the prices of goods (excluding bonds) and money stock in the 0-th period.

Assumption IX.1: The only economic unit which supplies labour is the labourer. The only economic unit which demands the labour is the firm.

IX.2: The only economic unit which receives dividends is the rentier.

IX.3: The labour which the k-th firm ($k=1,2, \ldots, \mu$) expects to be able to employ cannot be infinite after the 0-th period. That is, $y^k_{t,1} \geqq \bar{b}$ for a real number $\bar{b}$ such that

$$-\infty < \bar{b} < \sum_{i=1}^{h} b^i_t < 0 \quad (t=1,2, \ldots, \tau;\ t \neq 0).$$[50]

50. Notice that $t \neq 0$. This assumption implies that each firm knows that the labour supply is finite in each period. Also, this assumption ensures that the net

Assumption X : Each labourer supplies his labour in the 0-th period in the following way:

a) if the total *ex ante* supply of labour is greater than the total *ex ante* demand for labour, then each labourer revises his individual *ex ante* labour supply, even though all prices of goods (including labour and bonds) and money stock remain the same.

He revises his supply, taking into account the ratio of his *ex ante* labour supply to the total *ex ante* labour supply. To be exact his revised supply is equal to the total *ex ante* labour demand multiplied by the ratio of his individual *ex ante* labour supply to the total *ex ante* labour supply.

b) if the total *ex ante* supply of labour is smaller than the total *ex ante* demand for labour, then each labourer does not revise his labour supply as long as all prices of goods (including labour and bonds) and money stock remain the same. His labour supply is still the same as his individual *ex ante* labour supply.

This assumption is different from Clower's "dual-decision hypothesis" in that it takes into account the ratio of each individual's *ex ante* labour supply to the total *ex ante* labour supply. Fundamentally, however, our assumption can be regarded as the same as Clower's. Accordingly, we may safely call our assumption a dual-

---

output planned by the firm $y^k_{t,j}$ (k=1,2, ..., μ; t=1,2, ..., τ; j=2,3, ..., n) cannot be infinite, by virtue of Assumption III.4, *etc*. (Cf. Appendix I). Furthermore, this finiteness of the net output after the 0-th period is very important for the existence of the subjective equilibrium of each firm. This will become clear during the existence proof. The reason we exclude the 0-th period is that the infiniteness of net output is inherently ensured in the equilibrium. (Cf. p. 43 below.)

decision hypothesis.[51]

Let us make some comments on Assumption X. This assumption says that each labourer revises his labour supply so that his revised supply is equal to the total *ex ante* labour demand multiplied by the ratio of his individual *ex ante* supply to the total *ex ante* labour supply. However, the labourer himself is not, in fact, willing to make such a choice, but is obliged to make it. We should consider that today's market mechanism makes him choose such a ratio. We will not specify this mechanism here.

---

51. See pp. 1-4 above and Clower [2] pp. 118-120.

CHAPTER IV

THE EXISTENCE PROOF

In the following, we will try to prove the existence of a general equilibrium under the dual-decision hypothesis. The proof will proceed in four steps.

First, for convenience, we will rewrite the household's and firm's budget constraints and money constraints. Second, we will construct *ex ante* individual demand and supply functions which will then be adapted to the dual-decision hypothesis. Third, we will prove the existence of a general market equilibrium model, with modified functions, under the dual-decision hypothesis. Last, we will prove the existence of a general market equilibrium model, with unmodified functions, under the dual-decision hypothesis.

1. The Household's and Firm's Budget Constraints and Money Constraints Rewritten for Convenience

1.1 The Household's Budget Constraints and Money Constraints

Let $\lambda^i = \dfrac{\bar{x}^i_{o,o}}{\bar{Z}_o} \geqq 0$ $(i=1,2, \ldots, \ell)$ and $\lambda^k = \dfrac{\bar{y}^k_{o,o}}{\bar{Z}_o} \geqq 0$ $(k=1,2, \ldots, \mu)$. Of course, $\sum_{i=1}^{\ell}\lambda^i + \sum_{k=1}^{\mu}\lambda^k = 1$. Then, the labourer's budget constraints (2.i) become (2.i)' and the rentier's budget constraints (2.ii) become (2.ii)' and then (2.ii)''. The labourer's money constraints (2.i.a) become (2.i.a)', and the rentier's money constraints (2.ii.a) become (2.ii.a)'.

$$P_o x^i_o + P_{o,n+1} x^i_{o,n+1} + x^i_{o,o} \leqq \lambda^i \bar{Z}_o + P_o \bar{x}^i_o$$

$$P^i_1 x^i_1 + P^i_{1,n+1} x^i_{1,n+1} + x^i_{1,o} \leqq x^i_{o,n+1} + x^i_{o,o}$$

$$\text{(2.i)}' \qquad \cdots\cdots\cdots\cdots\cdots\cdots\cdots\cdots\cdots\cdots$$

$$P^i_\tau x^i_\tau \leqq x^i_{\tau-1,n+1} + x^i_{\tau-1,o}$$

$$x^i_{t,1} \leqq 0, \qquad t=0,1, \ldots, \tau;$$

$$i=1,2, \ldots, h.$$

$$P_o x_o^i + P_{o,n+1} x_{o,n+1}^i + x_{o,o}^i \leqq \lambda^i \bar{Z}_o + P_o \bar{x}_o^i + \sum_{k=1}^{\mu} \alpha_{o,k}^i \pi_{o,k}$$

$$P_1^i x_1^i + P_{1,n+1}^i x_{1,n+1}^i + x_{1,o}^i \leqq x_{o,n+1}^i + x_{o,o}^i + \sum_{k=1}^{\mu} \alpha_{1,k}^i \pi_{1,k}^i$$

(2.ii)' ....

$$P_\tau^i x_\tau^i \leqq x_{\tau-1,n+1}^i + x_{\tau-1,o}^i + \sum_{k=1}^{\mu} \alpha_{\tau,k}^i \pi_{\tau,k}^i$$

$$x_{t,1}^i = 0, \quad t=0,1, \ldots, \tau; \quad i=h+1,h+2, \ldots, \ell.$$

However, the rentier's budget constraints (2.ii)', which have already been rewritten, must again be rewritten as follows:.

$$P_o x_o^i + P_{o,n+1} x_{o,n+1}^i + x_{o,o}^i \leqq \lambda^i \bar{Z}_o + P_o \bar{x}_o^i + \max\left(\sum_{k=1}^{\mu} \alpha_{o,k}^i P_o y_o^k, 0\right)$$

(2.ii)'' $$P_1^i x_1^i + P_{1,n+1}^i x_{1,n+1}^i + x_{1,o}^i \leqq x_{o,n+1}^i + x_{o,o}^i + \sum_{k=1}^{\mu} \alpha_{1,k}^i \pi_{1,k}^i$$

....

$$P_\tau^i x_\tau^i \leqq x_{\tau-1,n+1}^i + x_{\tau-1,o}^i + \sum_{k=1}^{\mu} \alpha_{\tau,k}^i \pi_{\tau,k}^i$$

$$x_{t,1}^i = 0, \quad t=0,1, \ldots, \tau; \quad i=h+1,h+2, \ldots, \ell.$$

The reason why (2.ii)' must be rewritten as (2.ii)'' is that, although the term $\pi_{o,k}$ in the first inequality of (2.ii)' is single-valued for $P \in S^o$ or $P \in S^{\texttt{¤}}$,[52] this term is, in general, not single-valued for $P \in S$; and that this set S is ultimately adopted in the existence proof. On the other hand, $\pi_{o,k}$ is $P_o y_o^k$ by definition and y_o^k is to be originally determined by each firm's maximization behaviour, independently of each rentier's maximization behaviour. Accordingly, in order to complete our existence proof, we will demonstrate that, in an equilibrium, the y_o^k in the rentier's constraints is the same y_o^k as the one determined by the firm's

52. See P. 58 for the definition of $S^{\texttt{¤}}$.

maximization behaviour; and that, since $P_o y_o^k \geqq 0$, $\max(\sum_{k=1}^{\mu} \alpha_{o,k}^i P_o y_o^k, 0)$ becomes equal to $\sum_{k=1}^{\mu} \alpha_{o,k}^i P_o y_o^k$, *i.e.*, $\sum_{k=1}^{\mu} \alpha_{o,k}^i \pi_{o,k}$. Hence, (2.ii)'' returns, in a normalized equilibrium (*i.e.*, in the fixed point), to the budget constraints (2.ii)' and eventually, in a final equilibrium, to the set of original budget constraints (2.ii) itself.

Now, (2.i.a)' and (2.ii.a)' are as follows :

$$\sum_{j=2}^{n} \max\{P_{o,j}(x_{o,j}^i - \bar{x}_{o,j}^i), 0\} + \max(P_{o,n+1} x_{o,n+1}^i, 0)$$

$$\leqq \lambda^i \bar{Z}_o - \kappa_{o,1}^i P_{o,1} x_{o,1}^i + \sum_{j=2}^{n} \max\{\kappa_{o,j}^i P_{o,j}(\bar{x}_{o,j}^i - x_{o,j}^i), 0\}$$

$$+ \max(-\kappa_{o,n+1}^i P_{o,n+1} x_{o,n+1}^i, 0)$$

$$\text{(2.i.a)'} \quad \sum_{j=2}^{n} P_{1,j}^i x_{1,j}^i + \max(P_{1,n+1}^i x_{1,n+1}^i, 0) + \max(-x_{o,n+1}^i, 0)$$

$$\leqq x_{o,o}^i - \kappa_{1,1}^i P_{1,1}^i x_{1,1}^i + \max(\kappa_{o,b}^i x_{o,n+1}^i, 0)$$

$$+ \max(-\kappa_{1,n+1}^i P_{1,n+1}^i x_{1,n+1}^i, 0)$$

....

$$\sum_{j=2}^{n} P_{\tau,j}^i x_{\tau,j}^i + \max(-x_{\tau-1,n+1}^i, 0)$$

$$\leqq x_{\tau-1,o}^i - \kappa_{\tau,1}^i P_{\tau,1}^i x_{\tau,1}^i + \max(\kappa_{\tau-1,b}^i x_{\tau-1,n+1}^i, 0),$$

$$i=1,2,\ \ldots,\ h.$$

$$\sum_{j=2}^{n} \max\{P_{o,j}(x_{o,j}^i - \bar{x}_{o,j}^i), 0\} + \max(P_{o,n+1} x_{o,n+1}^i, 0)$$

$$\leqq \lambda^i \bar{Z}_o + \sum_{j=2}^{n} \max\{\kappa_{o,j}^i P_{o,j}(\bar{x}_{o,j}^i - x_{o,j}^i), 0\}$$

$$+ \max(-\kappa_{o,n+1}^i P_{o,n+1} x_{o,n+1}^i, 0)$$

$$\text{(2.ii.a)'} \quad \sum_{j=2}^{n} P_{1,j}^i x_{1,j}^i + \max(P_{1,n+1}^i x_{1,n+1}^i, 0) + \max(-x_{o,n+1}^i, 0)$$

$$\leqq x^i_{o,o} + \max(\kappa^i_{o,b} x^i_{o,n+1}, 0) + \max(-\kappa^i_{1,n+1} P^i_{1,n+1} x^i_{1,n+1}, 0)$$

....

$$\sum_{j=2}^{n} P^i_{\tau,j} x^i_{\tau,j} + \max(-x^i_{\tau-1,n+1}, 0)$$

$$\leqq x^i_{\tau-1,o} + \max(\kappa^i_{\tau-1,b} x^i_{\tau-1,n+1}, 0),$$

$$i=h+1, h+2, \ldots, \ell.$$

1.2 The Firm's Budget Constraints and Money Constraints

First, we will explicitly show that β^k is equal to $y^k_{\tau-1,o} + y^k_{\tau-1,n+1}$, although we have accepted it as so until now. If we look at the last inequality of the set of budget constraints (3), the firm's cash balance remaining at the end of the τ-th period, before profit is divided, is $y^k_{\tau-1,o} + y^k_{\tau-1,n+1} + \sum_{j=1}^{n} \max(P^k_{\tau,j} y^k_{\tau,j}, 0) - \sum_{j=1}^{n} \max(-P^k_{\tau,j} y^k_{\tau,j}, 0)$.[53]

Since $\pi^k_{\tau,k} = P^k_\tau y^k_\tau$ by definition, the cash remaining after profit has been divided β^k is $y^k_{\tau-1,o} + y^k_{\tau-1,n+1} + \sum_{j=1}^{n} \max(P^k_{\tau,j} y^k_{\tau,j}, 0) - \sum_{j=1}^{n} \max(-P^k_{\tau,j} y^k_{\tau,j}, 0) - P^k_\tau y^k_\tau$ and hence

$$\beta^k = y^k_{\tau-1,o} + y^k_{\tau-1,n+1}.$$

Since we have already imposed (3.d), the firm's budget constraints (3) become (3)' by definition of $\pi_{o,k}$ and $\pi^k_{t,k}$ $(t=1,2, \ldots, \tau)$,[54] and the firm's money constraints (3.a) become (3.a)'.

---

53. Note that (3), (3.a), *etc.* must be satisfied simultaneously.
54. Cf. p. 15 above.

$$P_{o,n+1}y^k_{o,n+1} + y^k_{o,o} \leqq \lambda^k \bar{Z}_o + P_o \bar{y}^k_o$$

(3)' $$P^k_{1,n+1}y^k_{1,n+1} + y^k_{1,o} \leqq y^k_{o,n+1} + y^k_{o,o}$$

....

$$P^k_{\tau-1,n+1}y^k_{\tau-1,n+1} + y^k_{\tau-1,o} \leqq y^k_{\tau-2,n+1} + y^k_{\tau-2,o},$$

$$k=1,2,\ \ldots,\ \mu.$$

$$\sum_{j=1}^{n}\max\{-P_{o,j}(y^k_{o,j} + \bar{y}^k_{o,j}),0\}$$

$$+ \max(P_{o,n+1}y^k_{o,n+1},0) \leqq \lambda^k \bar{Z}_o$$

$$+ \sum_{j\in I^k} P_{o,j}(\bar{\kappa}^k_{o,j}\bar{y}^k_{o,j} + \kappa^k_{o,j}y^k_{o,j})$$

$$+ \sum_{j\in \tilde{I}^k}\max\{\kappa^k_{o,j}P_{o,j}(\bar{y}^k_{o,j} + y^k_{o,j}),0\}$$

(3.a)' $$+ \max(-\kappa^k_{o,n+1}P_{o,n+1}y^k_{o,n+1},0)$$

$$\sum_{j=1}^{n}\max(-P^k_{1,j}y^k_{1,j},0) + \max(P^k_{1,n+1}y^k_{1,n+1},0)$$

$$+ \max(-y^k_{o,n+1},0) \leqq y^k_{o,o} + \sum_{j=1}^{n}\max(\kappa^k_{1,j}P^k_{1,j}y^k_{1,j},0)$$

$$+ \max(\kappa^k_{o,b}y^k_{o,n+1},0) + \max(-\kappa^k_{1,n+1}P^k_{1,n+1}y^k_{1,n+1},0)$$

....

$$\sum_{j=1}^{n}\max(-P^k_{\tau,j}y^k_{\tau,j},0) + \max(-y^k_{\tau-1,n+1},0)$$

$$\leqq y^k_{\tau-1,o} + \sum_{j=1}^{n}\max(\kappa^k_{\tau,j}P^k_{\tau,j}y^k_{\tau,j},0) + \max(\kappa^k_{\tau-1,b}y^k_{\tau-1,n+1},0),$$

$$k=1,2,\ \ldots,\ \mu.$$

2. Construction of Individual Demand or Supply Functions

Before investigating the market equilibrium, we must consider the subjective equilibrium. That is, we must construct each individual's demand and supply functions. First, we will construct each individual's *ex ante* demand and supply functions using household's and firm's modified choice sets which are obtained by restricting the original choice sets. Next, we will construct each individual's demand or supply functions adopting the dual-decision hypothesis, still using the modified choice sets.

2.1 Modified Individual *ex ante* Demand or Supply Functions

First, let us normalize $(P_{o,2}, P_{o,3}, \ldots, P_{o,n+1}, \bar{Z}_o)$ in the following way:

$$S_n = \{(P_{o,2}, P_{o,3}, \ldots, P_{o,n+1}, \bar{z}) \mid P_{o,j} \geqq 0 \quad (j=2,3, \ldots, n+1),$$

$$\bar{z} \geqq 0, \quad \sum_{j=2}^{n+1} P_{o,j} + \bar{z} = 1\},$$

where $(P_{o,2}, P_{o,3}, \ldots, P_{o,n+1}, \bar{z})$ denotes the normalized vector of $(P_{o,2}, P_{o,3}, \ldots, P_{o,n+1}, \bar{Z})$. This set S_n is an n-dimensional simplex, and hence convex and compact.

Obviously:

a) We have always the positive minimum wage $\bar{w}$ from Assumption VII. a) and c) for any $(P_{o,2}, P_{o,3}, \ldots, P_{o,n+1}, \bar{z}) \in S_n$,

b) by virtue of the compactness of S_n and Assumption VII. b), we can find a positive real number $\bar{w}'$ such that $\bar{w}' \leqq \bar{w} = W(P_{o,2}, P_{o,3}, \ldots, P_{o,n+1}, \bar{z})$ for any $(P_{o,1}, P_{o,2}, \ldots, P_{o,n+1}, \bar{z}) \in S_n$,

and

c) it is clear that $\hat{w} > \bar{w} = W(P_{o,2}, P_{o,3}, \ldots, P_{o,n+1}, \bar{z})$ for any $(P_{o,2}, P_{o,3}, \ldots, P_{o,n+1}, \bar{z}) \in S_n$, where $\hat{w}$ is defined in Assumption III.5.

Now, let S_o be the set:

$$S_o = \{P_{o,1} \mid \hat{w} \geqq P_{o,1} \geqq \bar{w}' > 0\}.$$

This set is also convex and compact.

Next, let S be the set $S = S_o \times S_n$ and S^o the set $S^o = S_o \times S_n^o$, where S_n^o is the interior of S_n.

Let

$$P = (P_{o,1}, P_{o,2}, \ldots, P_{o,n+1}, \bar{z}).$$

Then, any $P \in S^o$ is positive.

Some comments are in order on the economic meaning of construction of the sets S_n, S_o, and $S = (S_o \times S_n)$. First, the reason we are obliged to construct S_o and S_n separately is that there exists a minimum money wage in our economic system. Next, the reason why, in the existence proof, we employ the set S, where the money stock $\bar{Z}_o$ is normalized simultaneously with other prices, is that we should choose what Patinkin calls "the first valid dichotomy".[55] Although the set S itself is not a simplex, S_n is a simplex in that it consists of normalized vectors $(P_{o,2}, P_{o,3}, \ldots, P_{o,n+1}, \bar{z})$ where $\bar{z}$ is a normalized money stock. Moreover, from Assumption VII. a), $\bar{w}$ $(\in S_o)$ is a function of these normalized vectors, and due to Assumption VII. d), this function is homogeneous to degree one with respect to the variables excluding bond price. Therefore, we may regard S as a sort of simplex, although the sum of the elements of S is not 1. Such an S is suitable in order to correctly treat the problem of real cash balance.

Equilibrium quantities and normalized equilibrium prices found in the first procedure employing such an S are certainly <u>real</u> equilibrium prices (equilibrium ratios) and <u>real</u> equilibrium quantities (including <u>real</u> bond demands or supplies and <u>real</u> cash balances).

In the second procedure, shifting from the normalized equilibrium money stock $\bar{z}$ to the actual money stock $\bar{Z}_o$, nominal or absolute prices and quantities are determined simultaneously with <u>real</u> prices and quantities. Normalized equilibrium prices, excluding bond price, are shifted as much as the normalized equilibrium

---

55. We may call our procedure the dichotomy, because, as described in this text, two procedures are used in two stages. On the other hand, we preferred the first valid dichotomy to the second valid dichotomy, for reasons which will become evident in footnote 113. See Patinkin [22] *op. cit.*, pp. 171-186, and pp. 622-624 for the valid dichotomy.

money stock at the same time. Not the bond price, but bond demands or supplies are shifted as much as prices of other goods at the same time.

Now, if there is an equilibrium quantity of demand and supply in the standard general market equilibrium,[56] it satisfies (4) in the preceding chapter.

Next, we take the set of inequalities (6):

$$(6) \qquad \begin{aligned} &\sum_{i=1}^{\ell} x_o^i - \sum_{i=1}^{\ell} \bar{x}_o^i - \sum_{k=1}^{\mu} y_o^k - \sum_{k=1}^{\mu} \bar{y}_o^k \leqq 0, \\ &\sum_{i=1}^{\ell} x_{o,n+1}^i + \sum_{k=1}^{\mu} y_{o,n+1}^k \leqq 0, \\ &\sum_{i=1}^{\ell} x_{o,o}^i + \sum_{k=1}^{\mu} y_{o,o}^k - \bar{Z}_o \leqq 0, \end{aligned}$$

and consider all solutions of (6), *i.e.*,

$$(7) \qquad \begin{bmatrix} x_o^1, & x_o^2, & \ldots\ldots\ldots, & x_o^{\ell}, & y_o^1, & y_o^2, & \ldots\ldots\ldots, & y_o^{\mu} \\ x_{o,n+1}^1, & x_{o,n+1}^2, & \ldots, & x_{o,n+1}^{\ell}, & y_{o,n+1}^1, & y_{o,n+1}^2, & \ldots\ldots, & y_{o,n+1}^{\mu} \\ x_{o,o}^1, & x_{o,o}^2, & \ldots\ldots, & x_{o,o}^{\ell}, & y_{o,1}^1, & y_{o,o}^2, & \ldots\ldots\ldots, & y_{o,o}^{\mu} \end{bmatrix}.$$

For our existence proof, as stated above, it is first necessary to construct modified demand or supply functions, obtained by restricting choice sets, before we take up the true, or unmodified functions.[57] As a preliminary step in constructing the modified functions, we will define the sets of feasible vectors or scalars which satisfy (6) and verify the boundedness of these sets.

For each i (i=1,2, ..., ℓ), let L_o^i denote the set of those vector in D_o^i which appear as x_o^i in any of the solutions (7) of the set of inequalities (6). For each i, let $L_{o,o}^i$ denote the set of those scalars in R_+^1 which appear as $x_{o,o}^i$ in any of the

---

56. Cf. pp. 19-20 above.

57. The reason we first construct modified functions by restricting choice sets (preference fields or the set of production processes) is that we wish to ensure the existence of a maximum value for each household's utility and for each firm's "present value". Furthermore we wish to ensure the upper semi-continuity of demand or supply functions. In the last stage, by taking up original, or non-modified functions, we will justify our procedure of restricting choice sets.

solutions (7) of (6). For each labourer i (i=1,2, ..., h), let $L^i_{o,n+1}$ denote the set of those scalars in R^1 which appear as $x^i_{o,n+1}$ both in any of the solutions (7) of (6) and in any vector $(x^i_{o,n+1}, x^i_{o,o}, x^i_1, x^i_{1,n+1})$ which satisfies the second inequality of (2.i.a), subject to (2.i.b).[58] For each rentier i (i=h+1,h+2, ..., ℓ), let $L^i_{o,n+1}$ denote the set of those scalars in R^1 which appear as $x^i_{o,n+1}$ both in any of the solutions (7) of (6) and in any vector $(x^i_{o,n+1}, x^i_{o,o}, x^i_1, x^i_{1,n+1})$ which satisfied the second inequality of (2.ii.a)', subject to (2.ii.b).[59]

For each k (k=1,2, ..., μ), let T^k_o denote the set of those vectors in Q^k_o which appear as y^k_o in any of the solutions (7) of (6). For each k, let $T^k_{o,o}$ denote the set of those scalars in R^1_+ which appear as $y^k_{o,o}$ in any of the solutions (7) of (6).

---

58. $(x^i_{o,n+1}, x^i_{o,o}, x^i_1, x^i_{1,n+1})$, $(x^i_o, x^i_{o,n+1}, x^i_{o,o}, x^i_1, x^i_{1,n+1}, x^i_{1,o}, \ldots, x^i_\tau)$ and $(y^k_o, y^k_{o,n+1}, y^k_{o,o}, y^k_1, y^k_{1,n+1}, y^k_{1,o}, \ldots, y^k_\tau)$ can be called neither row vectors nor column vectors, because x^i_t's (t=0,1, ..., τ) and y^k_t's (t=0,1, ..., τ) are column vectors and other elements are scalars. However, $(x^i_{o,n+1}, x^i_{o,o}, x^i_1, x^i_{1,n+1})$, $(x^i_o, x^i_{o,n+1}, x^i_{o,o}, x^i_1, x^i_{1,n+1}, x^i_{1,o}, \ldots, x^i_\tau)$ and $(y^k_o, y^k_{o,n+1}, y^k_{o,o}, y^k_1, y^k_{1,n+1}, y^k_{1,o}, \ldots, y^k_\tau)$ can still be considered vectors. (See footnote 24 above.) If a reader prefers, he may treat them as column vectors $(x^{i'}_o, x^i_{o,n+1}, x^i_{o,o}, x^{i'}_1, x^i_{1,n+1}, x^i_{1,o}, \ldots, x^{i'}_\tau)'$ and $(y^{k'}_o, y^k_{o,n+1}, y^k_{o,o}, y^{k'}_1, y^k_{1,n+1}, y^k_{1,o}, \ldots, y^{k'}_\tau)'$ respectively, or as row vectors $(x^{i'}_o, x^i_{o,n+1}, x^i_{o,o}, x^{i'}_1, x^i_{1,n+1}, x^i_{1,o}, \ldots, x^{i'}_\tau)$ and $(y^{k'}_o, y^k_{o,n+1}, y^k_{o,o}, y^{k'}_1, y^k_{1,n+1}, y^k_{1,o}, \ldots, y^{k'}_\tau)$ respectively.

59. We should note that $x^i_{o,o}$ and x^i_1 which appear in the second inequality of (2.i.a)' and of (2.ii.a)', belong to $L^i_{o,o}$ and D^i_1 respectively. It should also be noted that prices appearing in this inequality depend on $P \in S$.

Noreover, we note that the definition of $L^i_{o,n+1}$ differs from that of L^i_o and $L^i_{o,o}$. This difference stems from our supposing that, unlike real goods (which are produced only with production factors) and money stock (which is assumed constant), bonds may be supplied without limit because there is no cost of production factors. See footnote 40.

For each k, let $T^k_{o,n+1}$ denote the set of those scalars in R^1 which appear as $y^k_{o,n+1}$ both in any of the solutions (7) of (6) and in any vector $(y^k_{o,n+1}, y^k_{o,o}, y^k_1, y^k_{1,n+1})$ which satisfies the second inequality of (3.a)', subject to (3.b) and (3.c).[60]

Now, the set of inequalities (6) is less restrictive than (4). If there exists an equilibrium solution $\hat{x}^i_o, \hat{x}^i_{o,n+1}, \hat{x}^i_{o,o}, \hat{y}^k_{o,n+1}, \hat{y}^k_{o,o}$, then obviously we have

$$\hat{x}^i_o \in L^i_o, \quad \hat{x}^i_{o,n+1} \in L^i_{o,n+1}, \quad \hat{x}^i_{o,o} \in L^i_{o,o}$$

and

$$\hat{y}^k_o \in T^k_o, \quad \hat{y}^k_{o,n+1} \in T^k_{o,n+1}, \quad \hat{y}^k_{o,o} \in T^k_{o,o}.$$

Now, we will state the properties of these sets.

Lemma I.

For each i and each k,

a) $L^i_o, L^i_{o,n+1}, L^i_{o,o}, T^k_o, T^k_{o,n+1}$, and $T^k_{o,o}$ are non-empty sets.

b) $L^i_o, L^i_{o,n+1}, L^i_{o,o}, T^k_o, T^k_{o,n+1}$, and $T^k_{o,o}$ are convex sets.

c) $L^i_o, L^i_{o,n+1}, L^i_{o,o}, T^k_o, T^k_{o,n+1}$, and $T^k_{o,o}$ are bounded sets.

Proof.

a) The non-emptiness of sets L^i_o and T^k_o is easily shown.[61] Also, the non-emptiness of the sets $L^i_{o,n+1}, T^k_{o,n+1}, L^i_{o,o}$, and $T^k_{o,o}$ is easily shown.

b) The convexity of the sets L^i_o and T^k_o was shown by Nikaido.[62] The convexity of the sets $L^i_{o,n+1}, L^i_{o,o}, T^k_{o,n+1}$, and $T^k_{o,o}$ can be easily shown also.[63]

---

60. It should be noted that any $y^k_{o,o}$ which appears in the second inequality of (3.a)' belongs to $T^k_{o,o}$.

61. We can find such a vector other than the zero vector.

62. Nikaido [17] p. 278.

63. See Appendix III for proof of the convexity of sets $L^i_{o,n+1}$ and $T^k_{o,n+1}$.

c) The boundedness of the sets L^i_o and T^k_o is proved using a technique similar to Nikaido's.[64] The boundedness of the sets $L^i_{o,o}$ and $T^k_{o,o}$ is easily derived from the finiteness of money stock (*i.e.*, $\bar{Z}_o$), and the non-negativity of the demand for money stock (*i.e.*, $x^i_{o,o}$) and $y^k_{o,o}$. However, the boundedness of sets $L^i_{o,n+1}$ and $T^k_{o,n+1}$ cannot be directly derived from the limitations on the ability to redeem bonds, *e.g.* from the budget constraints, which have been used by other writers.[65]

The boundedness of $L^i_{o,n+1}$ (i=1,2, ..., h) is shown relatively easily by using the money constraints of each labourer, taking into account Assumption V.3, $x^i_1 \in D^i_1$, and the boundedness of $L^i_{o,o}$ (i=1,2, ..., h). Without using the budget constraints, we intend to show the boundedness of $L^i_{o,n+1}$ (i=1,2, ..., h) with as few assumptions as possible. Our method is equally applicable to any rentier as well as any labourer.

Examine the second inequality of the labourer's money constraints (2.i.a)'. We need only consider the case where $\kappa^i_{1,n+1}P^i_{1,n+1}$ is not zero, because $x^i_{o,n+1}$ cannot be $-\infty$ when $\kappa^i_{1,n+1}P^i_{1,n+1}$ is zero. If $x^i_{o,n+1}$ is $-\infty$, then $x^i_{1,n+1}$ must be $-\infty$ too. Thus, from Assumption V.3, *i.e.*, (2.i.b) and the second inequality of (2.i.a)', the following inequalities are derived:

$$\begin{aligned} x^i_{o,o} - \kappa^i_{1,1}P^i_{1,1}x^i_{1,1} & \\ \geqq \sum_{j=2}^{n} P^i_{1,j}x^i_{1,j} &- x^i_{o,n+1}(1-\kappa^i_{1,n+1}P^i_{1,n+1}) \\ &- \kappa^i_{1,n+1}P^i_{1,n+1}(x^i_{o,n+1} - x^i_{1,n+1}); \end{aligned}$$

---

64. Assumption I.1 and Assumptions III.1, III.3, III.4 are employed in this proof. Cf. Nikaido *op. cit.*, pp. 277-280, and Nikaido [18], pp. 258-260.
65. Cf. footnote 40.

$$x^i_{o,o} - \kappa^i_{1,1}P^i_{1,1}x^i_{1,1}$$

(2.i.a)'(1)
$$\geqq \sum_{j=2}^{n} P^i_{1,j}x^i_{1,j} - x^i_{o,n+1}(1-\kappa^i_{1,n+1}P^i_{1,n+1})$$
$$- \kappa^i_{1,n+1}P^i_{1,n+1}\Delta.$$

Without loss of generality, the vector of the prices of goods (including labour and bonds) and money stock, *i.e.*, $P = (P_{o,1}, P_{o,2}, \ldots, P_{o,n+1}, \bar{z})$ can be assumed to belong to S.[66, 67]

Since $x^i_{o,o} \in L^i_{o,o}$, $x^i_1 \in D^i_1$ and since $P^i_{1,1}$ depends upon $P \in S$ where S is compact, $x^i_{o,o}$ and $-\kappa^i_{1,1}P^i_{1,1}x^i_{1,1}$ in the left-hand side have upper bounds.[68] It follows from Assumptions IV.4.c),VIII.1.c),and VIII.3 that $(1-\kappa^i_{1,n+1}P^i_{1,n+1})$ is positive.[69] Also, $\sum_{j=2}^{n} P^i_{1,j}x^i_{1,j} \geqq 0$. Accordingly, $x^i_{o,n+1}$ $(i=1,2, \ldots, h)$ cannot be $-\infty$. Also, we can easily find a lower bound of $x^i_{o,n+1}$ which is independent of the expected prices which depend on $P \in S$.[70]

---

66. Cf. pp. 39-40 above.

67. $P = (P_{o,1}, P_{o,2}, \ldots, P_{o,n+1}, \bar{z})$ is often considered to be a set of independent variables. In that case, for example, the functions ${}_tP^i_j$ and ${}_tP^k_j$ are rewritten without loss of generality as follows:

$$P^i_{t,j} = {}_tP^i_j(P_{o,1}, P_{o,2}, \ldots, P_{o,n+1}, \bar{x}^i_{o,o}) = {}_tP^i_j(P_{o,1}, P_{o,2}, \ldots, P_{o,n+1}, \lambda^i\bar{z}),$$

and

$$P^k_{t,j} = {}_tP^k_j(P_{o,1}, P_{o,2}, \ldots, P_{o,n+1}, \bar{y}^k_{o,o}) = {}_tP^k_j(P_{o,1}, P_{o,2}, \ldots, P_{o,n+1}, \lambda^k\bar{z}),$$

where λ^i and λ^k are constant.

Cf. pp. 30-31 and p. 34 above.

68. See footnote 69.

69. All $P^i_{1,j}$'s $(j=1,2, \ldots, n+1)$ have upper bounds, because the functions ${}_1P^i_j(j=1,2, \ldots, n+1)$ are single-valued and continuous due to Assumption VIII.3, and because S is compact. Also, $P^i_{1,n+1}$ is not larger than one by virtue of Assumption VIII.1.c).

70. Such a lower bound can be found as follows. Consider the following (2.i.a)'(1.α):

(2.i.a)'(1.α) $$\bar{\bar{x}}^i_{o,o} - \kappa^i_{1,1}\bar{\bar{P}}^i_{1,1}\underline{\underline{x}}^i_{1,1} \geqq - x^i_{o,n+1}(1-\kappa^i_{1,n+1}) - \kappa^i_{1,n+1}\Delta,$$

where $\bar{\bar{x}}^i_{o,o}$ is an upper bound of $L^i_{o,o}$, $\bar{\bar{P}}^i_{1,1}$ is the maximum of the positive

The same procedure holds for rentiers. For rentiers, we use (2.ii.b) and the second inequality of (2.ii.a)'.[71] For firms, on the other hand, we require another proof, one which employs Assumptions III.1, III.4, the money constraints (3.a)', and the inequality (6). The proof is somewhat intricate, but, we can still verify that $y^k_{o,n+1}$ has a lower bound.[72] That is,

$x^i_{o,n+1}(i=h+1,h+2, \ldots, \ell)$ and $y^k_{o,n+1}(k=1,2, \ldots, \mu)$ cannot be $-\infty$.

Therefore $x^i_{o,n+1}(i=1,2, \ldots, \ell)$ and $y^k_{o,n+1}(k=1,2, \ldots, \mu)$ also cannot be $+\infty$ because of (6).[73] Thus, $L^i_{o,n+1}$ is bounded for every household i and $T^k_{o,n+1}$ is bounded for every firm k.[74] (*Q.E.D.*)

---

expected wage in the 1st period (such a maximum exists due to the compactness of S and Assumption VIII.3), and $\underline{\underline{x}}^i_{1,1}$ is $b^i_{1,1}$ (cf. Assumption I.1). From this inequality we can directly find a lower bound of $x^i_{o,n+1}$. Let it be denoted by $\underline{\underline{x}}^i_{o,n+1}$. Then, all $x^i_{o,n+1}$'s$(i=1,2, \ldots, h)$ which satisfy (2.i.a)'(1) for any expected prices which depend on $P \in S$ are not less than $\underline{\underline{x}}^i_{o,n+1}(i=1,2, \ldots, h)$.

71. A lower bound of $x^i_{o,n+1}$ in the i-th rentier's case, *i.e.*, $\underline{\underline{x}}^i_{o,n+1}(i=h+1, h+2, \ldots, \ell)$, can be found in a way similar to that used in the labourer's case. (Cf. footnote 70.)

72. See Appendix I.

73. That $x^i_{o,n+1}(i=1,2, \ldots, \ell)$ and $y^k_{o,n+1}(k=1,2, \ldots, \mu)$ cannot be $+\infty$ is easily seen because $x^i_{o,n+1}(i=1,2, \ldots, h)$, $x^i_{o,n+1}(i=h+1,h+2, \ldots, \ell)$ and $y^k_{o,n+1}(k=1, 2, \ldots, \mu)$ must satisfy the following inequalities :

$$x^i_{o,n+1} \leqq \left| \sum_{i=1}^{h} \underline{\underline{x}}^i_{o,n+1} + \sum_{i=h+1}^{\ell} \underline{\underline{x}}^i_{o,n+1} + \sum_{k=1}^{\mu} \underline{\underline{y}}^k_{o,n+1} \right|, \quad i=1,2, \ldots, h;$$

$$x^i_{o,n+1} \leqq \left| \sum_{i=1}^{h} \underline{\underline{x}}^i_{o,n+1} + \sum_{i=h+1}^{\ell} \underline{\underline{x}}^i_{o,n+1} + \sum_{k=1}^{\mu} \underline{\underline{y}}^k_{o,n+1} \right|, \quad i=h+1,h+2, \ldots, \ell;$$

$$y^k_{o,n+1} \leqq \left| \sum_{i=1}^{h} \underline{\underline{x}}^i_{o,n+1} + \sum_{i=h+1}^{\ell} \underline{\underline{x}}^i_{o,n+1} + \sum_{k=1}^{\mu} \underline{\underline{y}}^k_{o,n+1} \right|, \quad k=1,2, \ldots, \mu.$$

74. If there is an equilibrium, for example, some $x^i_o \in L^i_o$, $x^i_{o,n+1} \in L^i_{o,n+1}$ and $x^i_{o,o} \in L^i_{o,o}$ must appear in some $(x^i_o, x^i_{o,n+1}, x^i_{o,o}, x^i_{1,1}, x^i_{1,n+1}, x^i_{1,o}, \ldots, x^i_T)$ which satisfies the household's constraints. This is different from Nikaido [17] pp. 277-280 in that he treats only goods (excluding bonds and money) in the 0-th period.

Note that these notations represent only the sets of vectors or scalars which satisfy (6). The boundedness of only these sets was verified. But, we must also take up the sets of vectors or scalars which satisfy all constraints of each economic unit in each period $t(=0,1, \ldots, \tau)$, as well. For this purpose we will define some additional notations and explain their topological properties. By employing some of these properties, we will verify the boundedness of the newly defined sets.[75]

Since L_o^i is bounded, we can select a compact hypercube V_o large enough to include L_o^i within its interior V_o^o :

$$V_o^o \supset L_o^i, \qquad i=1,2, \ldots, \ell.$$

Since $L_{o,n+1}^i$ and $L_{o,o}^i$ are bounded, we can also select a compact rectangle $\tilde{V}_o$ large enough to include the Cartesian product $L_{o,n+1}^i \times L_{o,o}^i$ within its interior $\tilde{V}_o^o$:

$$\tilde{V}_o^o \supset L_{o,n+1}^i \times L_{o,o}^i, \qquad i=1,2, \ldots, \ell.$$

Obviously,

$$D_o^i \supset L_o^i, \quad i=1,2, \ldots, \ell.$$

$$R^1 \times R_+^1 \supset L_{o,n+1}^i \times L_{o,o}^i, \qquad i=1,2, \ldots, \ell.$$

Form the intersection $B_o^i = D_o^i \cap V_o$ and the intersection $\tilde{B}_o^i = (R^1 \times R_+^1) \cap \tilde{V}_o$ for each i, $(i=1,2, \ldots, \ell)$.

As for T_o^k, we select a compact n-dimensional ball E_o, with center zero, large enough to include T_o^k within its interior E_o^o.[76] This selection is possible because of the boundedness of T_o^k :

---

75. The method we use to define these sets will entail some difficulty. This results mainly from the fact that our model treats only an equilibrium of the spot economy and not equilibria of futures markets.

76. See Dieudonné [3] p. 32 for explanation of the ball. The reason we select a ball and not a hypercube will become clear later. See pp. 60-61. This choice was suggested by a graduate student, Mr. H. Sato.

$$E_o^o \supset T_o^k, \qquad k=1,2, \ldots, \mu.$$

Needless to say,

$$Q_o^k \supset T_o^k, \qquad k=1,2, \ldots, \mu.$$

Because of the boundedness of $T^k_{o,n+1} \times T^k_{o,o}$, we can select a compact rectangle $\tilde{E}_o$ large enough to include $T^k_{o,n+1} \times T^k_{o,o}$ within its interior $\tilde{E}_o^o$:

$$\tilde{E}_o^o \supset T^k_{o,n+1} \times T^k_{o,o}, \qquad k=1,2, \ldots, \mu.$$

Form the intersection $A_o^k = Q_o^k \cap E_o$ and the intersection $\tilde{A}_o^k = (R^1 \times R^1_+) \cap \tilde{E}_o$ for each k.

Remark I.

A_o^k is compact and strictly convex, for each k.[77]

$\tilde{A}_o^k$ is compact and convex, for each k.

B_o^i is compact and convex, for each $i(i=1,2, \ldots, \ell)$.

$\tilde{B}_o^i$ is compact and convex, for each $i(i=1,2, \ldots, \ell)$.

Proof.

A_o^k is compact and strictly convex because Q_o^k is closed and strictly convex, and because E_o is compact and strictly convex. $\tilde{A}_o^k$ is compact and convex because $R^1 \times R^1_+$ is closed and convex, and because $\tilde{E}_o$ is compact and convex. B_o^i is compact and convex because D_o^i is closed and convex, and because V_o is compact and convex. $\tilde{B}_o^i$ is compact and convex because $R^1 \times R^1_+$ is closed and convex, and $\tilde{V}_o$ is compact and convex.[78] *(Q.E.D.)*

---

77. See Intriligator [11] p. 461 for the definition of strict convexity.
78. See Nikaido [17] p. 185 and his footnote * on p. 280.

Having verified the boundedness of sets $L^i_o, L^i_{o,n+1}, L^i_{o,o}, T^k_o, T^k_{o,n+1}$, and $T^k_{o,o}$, let us continue with our procedure.

For each labourer $i(i=1,2, \ldots, h)$ and each period $t(t=1,2, \ldots, \tau)$, let $\chi^i_t(P)$ denote the set of all x^i_t's in D^i_t that appear in any vector $(x^i_o, x^i_{o,n+1}, x^i_{o,o}, x^i_1, x^i_{1,n+1}, x^i_{1,o}, x^i_2, x^i_{2,n+1}, x^i_{2,o}, \ldots, x^i_\tau)$ which has the following properties :

for each given $P \in S$,

(i) this vector satisfies (2.i)', (2.i.a)', and (2.i.b), and

(ii) $(x^i_o, x^i_{o,n+1}, x^i_{o,o}) \in B^i_o \times \tilde{B}^i_o$.[79]

For each rentier $i(i=h+1,h+2, \ldots, \ell)$ and each period $t(t=1,2, \ldots, \tau)$, let $\chi^i_t(P, y^1_o, y^2_o, \ldots, y^\mu_o)$ denote the set of all x^i_t's in D^i_t that appear in any vector $(x^i_o, x^i_{o,n+1}, x^i_{o,o}, x^i_1, x^i_{1,n+1}, x^i_{1,o}, x^i_2, x^i_{2,n+1}, x^i_{2,o}, \ldots, x^i_\tau)$ which has the following properties :

for each given $(P, y^1_o, y^2_o, \ldots, y^\mu_o) \in S \times A_o$, where $A_o = A^1_o \times A^2_o \times \ldots \times A^\mu_o$,

(i) this vector satisfies (2.ii)", (2.ii.a)', and (2.ii.b), and

(ii) $(x^i_o, x^i_{o,n+1}, x^i_{o,o}) \in B^i_o \times \tilde{B}^i_o$.[80]

Let L^i_t denote $\chi^i_t(S)(i=1,2, \ldots, h)$ and $\chi^i_t(S \times A_o)(i=h+1,h+2, \ldots, \ell)$.[81]

---

79. For labourers, the boundedness of $\chi^i_t(S)$ defined below can be shown if only $x^i_{o,n+1}$ and $x^i_{o,o}$ belong to a bounded set $\tilde{B}^i_o$. The reason for this formulation is that x^i_o, *i.e.*, the subvectors of x^i, must be restricted within B^i_o as a step of our proof.

80. The reason we impose $(x^i_o, x^i_{o,n+1}, x^i_{o,o}) \in B^i_o \times \tilde{B}^i_o$ is stated in footnote 79. Also, the reason we form B^i_o as a rectangle and not as a ball is that we must ensure that, when the bond price in the 0-th period is zero, demand for such bonds by a rentier coming under Assumption IV.10 is infinite.

81. $\chi^i_t(S) = \bigcup_{P \in S} \chi^i_t(P)$,

$$\chi^i_t(S \times A_o) = \bigcup_{(P, y^1_o, y^2_o, \ldots, y^\mu_o) \in S \times A_o} \chi^i_t(P, y^1_o, y^2_o, \ldots, y^\mu_o).$$

For each labourer $i(i=1,2, \ldots, h)$ and each $t(t=1,2, \ldots, \tau-1)$, let $\chi^i_{t,n+1}(P)$ denote the set of all $x^i_{t,n+1}$'s in R^1 that appear in any vector $(x^i_o, x^i_{o,n+1}, x^i_{o,o}, x^i_1, x^i_{1,n+1}, x^i_{1,o}, x^i_2, x^i_{2,n+1}, x^i_{2,o}, \ldots, x^i_\tau)$ which has the following properties:

for each given $P \in S$

(i) this vector satisfies (2.i)', (2.i.a)', and (2.i.b), and

(ii) $(x^i_o, x^i_{o,n+1}, x^i_{o,o}) \in B^i_o \times \tilde{B}^i_o$.

For each rentier $i(i=h+1,h+2, \ldots, \ell)$ and each $t(t=1,2, \ldots, \tau-1)$, let $\chi^i_{t,n+1}(P, y^1_o, y^2_o, \ldots, y^\mu_o)$ denote the set of all $x^i_{t,n+1}$'s in R^1 that appear in any vector $(x^i_o, x^i_{o,n+1}, x^i_{o,o}, x^i_1, x^i_{1,n+1}, x^i_{1,o}, x^i_2, x^i_{2,n+1}, x^i_{2,o}, \ldots, x^i_\tau)$ which has the following properties:

for each given $(P, y^1_o, y^2_o, \ldots, y^\mu_o) \in S \times A_o$

(i) this vector satisfies (2.ii)", (2.ii.a)', and (2.ii.b), and

(ii) $(x^i_o, x^i_{o,n+1}, x^i_{o,o}) \in B^i_o \times \tilde{B}^i_o$.

Let $L^i_{t,n+1}$ denote $\chi^i_{t,n+1}(S)(i=1,2, \ldots, h)$ and $\chi^i_{t,n+1}(S \times A_o)(i=h+1,h+2, \ldots, \ell)$.

For each labourer $i(i=1,2, \ldots, h)$ and each $t(t=1,2, \ldots, \tau-1)$, let $\chi^i_{t,o}(P)$ denote the set of all $x^i_{t,o}$'s in R^1_+ that appear in any vector $(x^i_o, x^i_{o,n+1}, x^i_{o,o}, x^i_1, x^i_{1,n+1}, x^i_{1,o}, \ldots, x^i_\tau)$ which has the following properties:

for each given $P \in S$,

(i) this vector satisfies (2.i)', (2.i.a)', and (2.i.b), and

(ii) $(x^i_o, x^i_{o,n+1}, x^i_{o,o}) \in B^i_o \times \tilde{B}^i_o$.

For each rentier $i(i=h+1,h+2, \ldots, \ell)$ and each $t(t=1,\ldots,\tau-1)$, let $\chi^i_{t,o}(P, y^1_o, y^2_o, \ldots, y^\mu_o)$ denote the set of all $x^i_{t,o}$'s in R^1_+ that appear in any vector $(x^i_o, x^i_{o,n+1}, x^i_{o,o}, x^i_1, x^i_{1,n+1}, x^i_{1,o}, x^i_2, x^i_{2,n+1}, x^i_{2,o}, \ldots, x^i_\tau)$ which has the following properties:

for each given $(P, y_o^1, y_o^2, \ldots, y_o^\mu) \in S \times A_o$

(i) this vector satisfies (2.ii)", (2.ii.a)', and (2.ii.b), and

(ii) $(x_o^i, x_{o,n+1}^i, x_{o,o}^i) \in B_o^i \times \tilde{B}_o^i$.

Let $L_{t,o}^i$ denote $\chi_{t,o}^i(S)(i=1,2, \ldots, h)$ and $\chi_{t,o}^i(S \times A_o)(i=h+1,h+2, \ldots, \ell)$.

For firms as well, we will take steps similar to those taken for households (labourers and rentiers).

Now, for each firm k and each period t, let $T_t^k(P)$ denote the set of all y_t^k's in Q_t^k that appear in any vector $(y_o^k, y_{o,n+1}^k, y_{o,o}^k, y_1^k, y_{1,n+1}^k, y_{1,o}^k, y_2^k, y_{2,n+1}^k, y_{2,o}^k, \ldots, y_\tau^k)$ which has the following properties:

for each given $P \in S$,

(i) this vector satisfies (3)', (3.a)', (3.b), (3.c), and (3.d), and

(ii) $(y_o^k, y_{o,n+1}^k, y_{o,o}^k) \in A_o^k \times \tilde{A}_o^k$.[82]

Let T_t^k denote $T_t^k(S)$.

For each firm k and each period $t(t=1,2, \ldots, \tau-1)$, let $T_{t,n+1}^k(P)$ denote the set of all $y_{t,n+1}^k$'s in R^1 that appear in any vector $(y_o^k, y_{o,n+1}^k, y_{o,o}^k, y_1^k, y_{1,n+1}^k, y_{1,o}^k, y_2^k, y_{2,n+1}^k, y_{2,o}^k, \ldots, y_\tau^k)$ which has the following properties:

for each given $P \in S$,

(i) this vector satisfies (3)', (3.a)', (3.b), (3.c), and (3.d), and

(ii) $(y_o^k, y_{o,n+1}^k, y_{o,o}^k) \in A_o^k \times \tilde{A}_o^k$.

Let $T_{t,n+1}^k$ denote $T_{t,n+1}^k(S)$.

---

82. In order to show that $T_t^k(S)$ is bounded, we need only impose $(y_{o,n+1}^k, y_{o,o}^k) \in \tilde{A}_o^k$. The reason for this formulation is that y_o^k must be restricted within A_o^k as a step of our proof.

For each firm k and each period $t(t=1,2, \ldots, \tau-1)$, let $T_{t,o}(P)$ denote the set of all $y^k_{t,o}$'s in R^l_+ that appear in any vector $(y^k_o, y^k_{o,n+1}, y^k_{o,o}, y^k_1, y^k_{1,n+1}, y^k_{1,o}, y^k_2, y^k_{2,n+1}, y^k_{2,o}, \ldots, y^k_\tau)$ which has the following properties:

for each given $P \in S$,

(i) this vector satisfies (3)', (3.a)', (3.b), (3.c), and (3.d), and

(ii) $(y^k_o, y^k_{o,n+1}, y^k_{o,o}) \in A^k_o \times \tilde{A}^k_o$.

Let $T^k_{t,o}$ denote $T^k_{t,o}(S)$.

We will examine the boundedness of sets $L^i_t, T^k_t, L^i_{t,n+1}, T^k_{t,n+1}, L^i_{t,o}$ and $T^k_{t,o}$.

Lemma II.

For each i and each k,

L^i_t and T^k_t are bounded sets, $t=1,2, \ldots, \tau$.

$L^i_{t,n+1}$ and $T^k_{t,n+1}$ are bounded sets, $t=1,2, \ldots, \tau-1$.

$L^i_{t,o}$ and $T^k_{t,o}$ are bounded sets, $t=1,2, \ldots, \tau-1$.

Proof.

The boundedness of $L^i_{t,n+1} (i=1,2, \ldots, h)$ is derived from the compactness of $\tilde{B}^i_o$ and from (2.i.b) for each labourer i. The boundedness of $L^i_{t,n+1} (i=h+1,h+2, \ldots, \ell)$ is derived from the compactness of $\tilde{B}^i_o$ and from (2.ii.b) for each rentier i. The boundedness of $T^k_{t,n+1}$ is derived from the compactness of $\tilde{A}^k_o$ and from (3.b) for each firm k.

Next, the boundedness of $L^i_t, L^i_{t,o}, T^k_t$, and $T^k_{t,o}$ are shown as follows. As a consequence of Assumption VIII.1, for each i and each k,

$$P^i_{t,j} = {}_tP^i_j(P) > 0$$

and

$$p^k_{t,j} = {}_tP^k_j(P) > 0 \quad \text{for any } P \in S,$$

$$t=1,2, \ldots, \tau;\ j=1,2, \ldots, n.$$

Also, it is clear, from the continuity of these functions (cf. Assumption VIII.3) and from the compactness of S, that the functions ${}_tP^i_j$ and ${}_tP^k_j$ take a maximum and a minimum on S. That is, there exist a maximum expected price and a minimum expected price which are both positive. The proof will be established by a successive method.

For example, the boundedness of $L^i_1(i=1,2, \ldots, h)$ and $L^i_{1,o}(i=1,2, \ldots, h)$ can be derived from (2.i)', making use of the boundedness of the positive expected prices, the lower boundedness of $D^i_1(i=1,2, \ldots, h)$, the boundedness of $\tilde{B}^i_o$ and $L^i_{1,n+1}(i=1,2, \ldots, h)$, and Assumption VIII.2. The boundedness of L^i_2 and $L^i_{2,o}$ can be derived from (2.i)', making use of the boundedness of the positive expected prices, the lower boundedness of D^i_2, the boundedness of $L^i_{t,n+1}(t=1,2)$ and $L^i_{1,o}$, and Assumption VIII.2. By applying the same method successively to each period after the 2nd period, the boundedness of $L^i_t(t=3, 4, \ldots, \tau)$ and $L^i_{t,o}(t=3,4, \ldots, \tau-1)$ can be shown.[83] Similarly, the boundedness of $L^i_t(i=h+1,h+2, \ldots, \ell;\ t=1,2, \ldots, \tau)$ and $L^i_{t,o}(i=h+1,h+2, \ldots, \ell;\ t=1,2, \ldots, \tau-1)$ can be derived from (2.ii)", making use of the boundedness

---

83. It may seem that $L^i_t(=\chi^i_t(S))$ is unbounded despite the compactness of the image $\chi^i_t(P)$. However, such a problem cannot arise in this case. Suppose that some x^i_t belonging to L^i_t can be $+\infty$. Then we have a sequence of vectors $\{x^\nu_t\}$ such that, for some element, say $x^\nu_{t,j}(>0)$, $\lim_{\nu\to\infty} x^\nu_{t,j} = +\infty$. However, this is impossible because the minimum value, of all the values which $P^i_{t,j}$ can take, is positive, because $x^i_t \in D^i_t$ and because $L^i_{t-1,n+1}, L^i_{t,n+1}$ and $L^i_{t-1,o}$ are bounded. That is, x^ν_t violates

of the positive expected prices and that of the non-negative expected dividend,[84] the boundedness of $\tilde{B}_o^i$ and $L_{t,n+1}^i(t=1,2, \ldots, \tau-1)$, and Assumption VIII.2.

The boundedness of $T_t^k(t=1,2, \ldots, \tau)$ can be clearly derived from the boundedness of net output and net input.[85] Also, by employing the same successive method, the boundedness of $T_{t,o}^k(k=1,2, \ldots, \mu;\ t=1,2, \ldots, \tau-1)$ can be derived from (3)', making use of the boundedness of $\tilde{A}_o^k$ and $T_{t,n+1}^k(t=1,2, \ldots, \tau-1)$, and Assumption VIII.2. *(Q.E.D.)*

Let L^i denote the Cartesian product $L_o^i \times L_{o,n+1}^i \times L_{o,o}^i \times L_1^i \times L_{1,n+1}^i \times L_{1,o}^i \times \ldots\ldots \times L_\tau^i$ and let T^k denote the Cartesian product $T_o^k \times T_{o,n+1}^k \times T_{o,o}^k \times T_1^k \times T_{1,n+1}^k \times T_{1,o}^k \times \ldots\ldots \times T_\tau^k$.

As we did for V_o, for each $t(t=1,2, \ldots, \tau)$, form a compact hypercube V_t large enough to include L_t^i within its interior V_t^o. This is possible because L_t^i is bounded. Thus,

$$V_t^o \supset L_t^i, \quad i=1,2, \ldots, \ell; \quad t=1,2, \ldots, \tau.$$

As we did for $\tilde{V}_o$, for each $t(t=1,2, \ldots, \tau-1)$, form a compact rectangle $\tilde{V}_t$ large enough to include the Cartesian product $L_{t,n+1}^i \times L_{t,o}^i$ within its interior $\tilde{V}_t^o$:

$$\tilde{V}_t^o \supset L_{t,n+1}^i \times L_{t,o}^i, \quad i=1,2, \ldots, \ell; \quad t=1,2, \ldots, \tau-1.$$

---

the t+1-th inequality of (2.i)' for $\nu \geqq \nu^o$, where ν represents the ν-th term of the sequence and ν^o is a sufficiently large number.

84. The boundedness of the expected dividend is derived from Assumption VI.3 and the compactness of S.

85. The boundedness of net output and net input is proved in Appendix I.

Let V denote the Cartesian product $V_o \times \tilde{V}_o \times V_1 \times \tilde{V}_1 \times V_2 \times \tilde{V}_2 \times \ldots\ldots \times V_\tau$ and let M^i denote the Cartesian product $D_o^i \times R^1 \times R_+^1 \times D_1^i \times R^1 \times R_+^1 \times D_2^i \times R^1 \times R_+^1 \times \ldots\ldots \times D_\tau^i$ for each $i(i=1,2, \ldots, \ell)$. Also, let V^o denote the interior of V. Then:

(8.i) $\quad V^o \supset L^i, \quad i=1,2, \ldots, \ell.$

(8.ii) $\quad M^i \supset L^i, \quad i=1,2, \ldots, \ell.$

As we did for E_o, for each $t(t=1,2, \ldots, \tau)$, form an n-dimensional compact ball E_t, with center zero, large enough to include T_t^k within its interior E_t^o. This is possible because of the boundedness of T_t^k.

Also, as we did for $\tilde{E}_o$, for each $t(t=1,2, \ldots, \tau-1)$ form a compact rectangle $\tilde{E}_t$ large enough to include $T_{t,n+1}^k \times T_{t,o}^k$ within its interior $\tilde{E}_t^o$. This is possible because of the boundedness of $T_{t,n+1}^k \times T_{t,o}^k$. Obviously:

$$E_t^o \supset T_t^k, \quad k=1,2, \ldots, \mu;\ t=1,2, \ldots, \tau.$$

$$\tilde{E}_t^o \supset T_{t,n+1}^k \times T_{t,o}^k, \quad k=1,2, \ldots, \mu;\ t=1,2, \ldots, \tau-1.$$

Let E denote the Cartesian product $E_o \times \tilde{E}_o \times E_1 \times \tilde{E}_1 \times E_2 \times \tilde{E}_2 \times \ldots\ldots \times E_\tau$, and let N^k denote the Cartesian product $Q_o^k \times R^1 \times R_+^1 \times Q_1^k \times R^1 \times R_+^1 \times Q_2^k \times R^1 \times R_+^1 \times Q_3^k \times \ldots\ldots \times Q_\tau^k$. Moreover, let E^o denote the interior of E. Then:

(8.iii) $\quad E^o \supset T^k, \quad k=1,2, \ldots, \mu.$

(8.iv) $\quad N^k \supset T^k, \quad k=1,2, \ldots, \mu.$

Let, A_t^k denote the intersection $Q_t^k \cap E_t$ and let $\tilde{A}_t^k$ denote the intersection $(R^1 \times R_+^1) \cap \tilde{E}_t$:

$$A_t^k = Q_t^k \cap E_t, \quad k=1,2, \ldots, \mu;\ t=1,2, \ldots, \tau.$$

$$\tilde{A}_t^k = (R^1 \times R_+^1) \cap \tilde{E}_t, \quad k=1,2, \ldots, \mu;\ t=1,2, \ldots, \tau-1.$$

Next, let B_t^i denote the intersection $D_t^i \cap V_t$ and let $\tilde{B}_t^i$ denote the intersection $(R^1 \times R_+^1) \cap \tilde{V}_t$:

$$B_t^i = D_t^i \cap V_t, \quad i=1,2, \ldots, \ell; \; t=1,2, \ldots, \tau.$$

$$\tilde{B}_t^i = (R^1 \times R_+^1) \cap \tilde{V}_t, \quad i=1,2, \ldots, \ell; \; t=1,2, \ldots, \tau.$$

Remark II.

A_t^k is compact and strictly convex, for each k and each t(t=0,1, ..., τ).

$\tilde{A}_t^k$ is compact and convex, for each k and each t(t=0,1,2, ..., τ-1).

B_t^i is compact and convex, for each i(i=1,2, ..., ℓ) and each t(t=0, 1, ..., τ).

$\tilde{B}_t^i$ is compact and convex, for each i(i=1,2, ..., ℓ) and each t(t=0, 1, ..., τ-1).

Since the proofs are the same as those for $A_o^k, \tilde{A}_o^k, B_o^i$, and $\tilde{B}_o^i$ in Remark I, they will be omitted.

If we let A^k denote the Cartesian product $A_o^k \times \tilde{A}_o^k \times A_1^k \times \tilde{A}_1^k \times A_2^k \times \tilde{A}_2^k \times \ldots\ldots \times A_\tau^k$, then by definition, for each k,

$$\begin{aligned} A^k &= (Q_o^k \cap E_o) \times \{(R^1 \times R_+^1) \cap \tilde{E}_o\} \times (Q_1^k \cap E_1) \times \{(R^1 \times R_+^1) \cap \tilde{E}_1\} \times \\ &\quad (Q_2^k \cap E_2) \times \{(R^1 \times R_+^1) \cap \tilde{E}_2\} \times \ldots\ldots \times (Q_\tau^k \cap E_\tau) \\ &= (Q_o^k \times R^1 \times R_+^1 \times Q_1^k \times R^1 \times R_+^1 \times Q_2^k \times R^1 \times R_+^1 \times \ldots\ldots \times Q_\tau^k) \cap \\ &\quad (E_o \times \tilde{E}_o \times E_1 \times \tilde{E}_1 \times E_2 \times \tilde{E}_2 \times \ldots\ldots \times E_\tau) \\ &= N^k \cap E. \end{aligned} \tag{9.i}$$

If we let B^i denote the Cartesian product $B_o^i \times \tilde{B}_o^i \times B_1^i \times \tilde{B}_1^i \times B_2^i \times \tilde{B}_2^i \times \ldots\ldots \times B_\tau^i$, then by definition, for each i(i=1,2, ..., ℓ),

$$B^i = (D_o^i \cap V_o) \times \{(R^1 \times R_+^1) \cap \tilde{V}_o\} \times (D_1^i \cap V_1) \times \{(R^1 \times R_+^1) \cap \tilde{V}_1\} \times$$

$$(D_2^i \cap V_2) \times \{(R^1 \times R_+^1) \cap \tilde{V}_2\} \times \ldots\ldots \times (D_\tau^i \cap V_\tau)$$

(9.ii) $$= (D_o^i \times R^1 \times R_+^1 \times D_1^i \times R^1 \times R_+^1 \times D_2^i \times R^1 \times R_+^1 \times \ldots\ldots \times D_\tau^i) \cap$$

$$(V_o \times \tilde{V}_o \times V_1 \times \tilde{V}_1 \times V_2 \times \tilde{V}_2 \times \ldots\ldots \times V_\tau)$$

$$= M^i \cap V.$$

Remark III.

A^k is non-empty, compact, and convex, for each k.

B^i is non-empty, compact, and convex, for each i(i=1,2, ..., ℓ).

Proof.

The non-emptiness of B^i and A^k is easily verified as follows.

For each i(i=1,2, ..., ℓ), and each k, take $(n+2)\tau$ + n-dimensional zero vectors of the i-th household and the k-th firm simultaneously. The first n+2-dimensional subvectors of these zero vectors are solutions of (6). By Assumptions I.1 and III.1, $0 \in D_t^i$, $0 \in Q_t^k$(t=0,1, ..., τ). Also, for each $P \in S$, $(n+2)\tau$ + n-dimensional zero vectors satisfy the constraints (2.i)', (2.i.a)', and (2.i.b) for the i-th labourer (i=1,2, ..., h), (2.ii)", (2.ii.a)', and (2.ii.b) for the i-th rentier (i=h+1,h+2, ..., ℓ), and (3)', (3.a)', (3.b), (3.c), and (3.d) for the k-th firm, respectively. Therefore, these zero vectors, *i.e.*, the i-th household's vector and the k-th firm's vector, belong to V and E, respectively. Obviously they belong also to M^i and N^k, respectively. Hence, they belong to B^i and A^k, respectively. Thus, B^i and A^k are non-empty sets. Since A^k and B^i are the Cartesian products of compact and convex sets by definition,[86] A^k and B^i are compact and convex.[87]

(*Q.E.D.*)

---

86. See p. 56.
87. See Nikaido [17], p. 197.

Last, we will define the following vectors x^i and y^k :

$$x^i = [x^i_o, x^i_{o,n+1}, x^i_{o,o}, x^i_1, x^i_{1,n+1}, x^i_{1,o}, \ldots, x^i_\tau]$$

$$y^k = [y^k_o, y^k_{o,n+1}, y^k_{o,o}, y^k_1, y^k_{1,n+1}, y^k_{1,o}, \ldots, y^k_\tau].$$

2.1.1 Modified *ex ante* Demand or Supply Functions of Individual Firms

Now we are ready to define demand or supply functions of firms by restricting the original choice sets of the profit maximization problem within the set A^k.

Let S^π be the set $S^\pi = S_o \times S^\pi_n$ where $S^\pi_n = \{(P_{o,2}, P_{o,3}, \ldots, P_{o,n+1}, \bar{z}) | P_{o,j} > 0$ $(j=2,3, \ldots, n+1)$, $\bar{z} \geqq 0$ and $\sum_{j=2}^{n+1} P_{o,j} + \bar{z} = 1\}$.[88]

Let us consider the k-th firm's individual demand or supply funciton. First, define $\Omega^k(P)$ by (10.i) :

(10.i) $\Omega^k(P) = \{y^k | y^k =$ maximizer of (1.iii), subject to (3)', (3.a)', (3.b), (3.c), (3.d), and $y^k \in A^k\}$, for each $P \in S^\pi$.

Then, let us investigate the following mapping which associates a set $\Omega^k(P)$ in A^k with each vector P on S^π, that is,

(10.ii) $P \to \Omega^k(P) : S^\pi \to A^k, \quad k=1,2, \ldots, \mu.$

We will prove below that the mapping Ω^k is closed. In order to prove it we will show the continuity of the following mapping :

(10.iii) $P \to \Omega^k_f(P) : S^\pi \to A^k, \quad k=1,2, \ldots, \mu,$

where $\Omega^k_f(P)$ is the set of feasible solutions, y^k, which belong to A^k of (3)', (3.a)', (3.b), (3.c), and (3.d) for each given $P \in S^\pi$.

---

88. S^π contains a vector $P = (P_{o,1}, P_{o,2}, \ldots, P_{o,n+1}, \bar{z})$ with $\bar{z} = 0$. The

The mapping Ω_f^k is continuous on S^{π}. That is, Ω_f^k is upper semi-continuous and lower semi-continuous. The upper semi-continuity of Ω_f^k is due to the closedness of Ω_f^k and the compactness of A^k.[89] The lower semi-continuity of Ω_f^k can be easily shown, also. This is because it follows from Assumption II.3 and IV.6 that, for each $P \in S^{\pi}$, there exists at least one vector y^k which belong to A^k and satisfies the inequalities (3)',(3.a)', and (3.d) in strict inequality, as well as the inequalities (3.b) and (3.c), not necessarily in strict inequality.[90] Thus, Ω_f^k is continuous. On the other hand, $\Pi_{o,k}$ of (1.iii) is also a continuous numerical function on $S^{\pi} \times A^k$ by virtue of Assumption VIII.3. Moreover, the image $\Omega_f^k(P)$ for each $P \in S^{\pi}$ is non-empty. Consequently, by virtue of Berge's Maximum theorem, the mapping Ω^k of (10.ii) is closed.[91] (*Q.E.D.*)

Also, this mapping is, in general, a multi-valued mapping.

Now, for each $y^k = (y_o^k, y_{o,n+1}^k, y_{o,o}^k, y_1^k, y_{o,n+1}^k, y_{1,o}^k, \ldots, y_T^k) \in \Omega^k(P)$, let

$$y_*^k = (y_o^k, y_1^k, \ldots, y_T^k).$$

We will call this y_*^k the subvector of y^k.[92] Now, let

$$\Omega_*^k(P) = \{y_*^k | y^k \in \Omega^k(P),\ y_*^k \in A_*^k\} \text{ for each } P \in S^{\pi},$$

$$\text{where } A_*^k = A_o^k \times A_1^k \times A_2^k \times .. \times A_T^k.$$

---

economic meaning of the case where $\bar{z} = 0$ will be explained below; footnote 113 on pp. 70-71.

89. See Berge [1] pp. 111-112, or Haga and Otsuki [10], pp. 122-123.

90. The lower semi-continuity of Ω_f^k is ensured if there exists such a vector y^k as stated above. (See Haga and Otsuki, *op.cit.* pp. 122-123, cf. Appendix II.)

91. See "Maximum theorem" in Berge [1], pp. 115-117, or Haga and Otsuki [10], pp. 122-123, for the topological properties of optimal solutions and the optimal value of the maximization problem.

92. y_*^k is a vector of the quantities of real goods other than bonds and money stock.

Then Ω_*^k can be considered to be a mapping which associates the set $\Omega_*^k(P)$ in A_*^k with each $P \in S^\mu$:

$$(10.\text{iv}) \qquad P \to \Omega_*^k(P) \; ; \; S^\mu \to A_*^k, \quad k=1,2, \ldots, \mu.$$

The mapping Ω_*^k is single-valued and continuous.[93] The single-valuedness of Ω_*^k can be verified as follows. If Ω_*^k is not single-valued, then there exist two different vectors $y_*^{k^1}$ and $y_*^{k^2}$, where $y_*^{k^1} \in \Omega_*^k(P)$ and $y_*^{k^2} \in \Omega_*^k(P)$. By definition of $y_*^{k^1}$ and $y_*^{k^2}$, there exist two different maximum solutions y^{k^1} and y^{k^2} which have $y_*^{k^1}$ and $y_*^{k^2}$ as their subvectors, respectively.[94] Now, form a convex linear combination of y^{k^1} and y^{k^2}, *i.e.* $y^k(\lambda) = \lambda y^{k^1} + (1 - \lambda)y^{k^2}$ where $0 < \lambda < 1$. Obviously, $y^k(\lambda) \in A^k$. It is also clear that $y^k(\lambda)$ satisfies (3)',(3.b),(3.c), and (3.d). This $y^k(\lambda)$ also satisfies the non-linear inequalities (3.a)', as can be easily verified by making use of Appendix III, which states the convexity of the set of feasible solutions of the non-linear inequalities (3.a)', *etc.*[95]

Suppose that $y_t^{k^1}$ and $y_t^{k^2}$, which are the subvectors of $y_*^{k^1}$ and $y_*^{k^2}$ respectively, are different in the $\tilde{t}$-th period. By virtue of the strict convexity of $A_t^k(t=0,1, \ldots, \tilde{t}, \ldots, \tau)$(cf. Remarks I,II), we can find a $y_{\tilde{t}}^{k'''}$ such that $y_{\tilde{t}}^{k'''} \geq \lambda y_{\tilde{t}}^{k^1} + (1 - \lambda)y_{\tilde{t}}^{k^2}$, where $y_{\tilde{t}}^{k'''} \in A_{\tilde{t}}^k$ and $0 < \lambda < 1$. Let us form the following new vector $y^{k^3}(\lambda)$: $y_t^{k^3}(\lambda) = \lambda y_t^{k^1} + (1 - \lambda)y_t^{k^2}$ for all t's other than $\tilde{t}$, $y_{\tilde{t}}^{k^3}(\lambda) = y_{\tilde{t}}^{k'''}$, $y_{t,n+1}^{k^3}(\lambda) = \lambda y_{t,n+1}^{k^1} + (1 - \lambda)y_{t,n+1}^{k^2}$ for each $t(t=0,1, \ldots, \tau-1)$, and $y_{t,o}^{k^3}(\lambda) =$

---

93. Ω_*^k is concerned with only real goods other than bonds and money stock.
94. Cf. p. 59.
95. See Appendix III pp. 110-111.

$\lambda y^{k^1}_{t,o} + (1-\lambda)y^{k^2}_{t,o}$ for each $t(t=0,1, \ldots, \tau-1)$. It is also clear that $y^{k^3}(\lambda)$ satisfies (3)',(3.b),(3.c), and (3.d). Moreover, we can see by a simple calculation $y^{k^3}(\lambda)$ satisfies the non-linear inequalities (3.a)'. Hence, $y^{k^3}(\lambda)$ satisfies all constraints. Thus, $y^{k^3}(\lambda)$ generates a greater present value for each $P \in S^{\sqcap}$ by virtue of Assumptions VIII.1.a), b) and VIII.2. Thus, the existence of two different vectors $y^{k^1}_*$ and $y^{k^2}_*$ is impossible. Hence, Ω^k_* is single-valued. The continuity of Ω^k_* is easily shown as follows. The mapping Ω^k_* of (10.iv) is the composition $\tilde{\Omega}^k \cdot \Omega^k$ of the upper semi-continuous mapping $\Omega^k(P \rightarrow \Omega^k : S^{\sqcap} \rightarrow A^k)$ and the projection, *i.e.*, a single-valued continuous mapping $\tilde{\Omega}^k(y^k \rightarrow \tilde{\Omega}^k(y^k) : A^k \rightarrow A^k_*)$. That is,

$$P \rightarrow \Omega^k_*(P) : S^{\sqcap} \rightarrow A^k_* = P \rightarrow \tilde{\Omega}^k(\Omega^k(P)) : S^{\sqcap} \rightarrow A^k_*.$$

Thus, by virtue of the theorem of composition of mappings, Ω^k_* is upper semi-continuous.[96] Moreover, Ω^k_* is single-valued, as we have shown. Accordingly, Ω^k_* is continuous. (*Q.E.D.*)

The closed mapping Ω^k can be extended to a closed mapping η^k from $S(\supset S^{\sqcap})$ into A^k.[97] We define $\eta^k(P)$ by (10.v) :

$$\text{(10.v)} \qquad \eta^k(P) = \{y^k \mid y^k \in A^k,\ (P,y^k) \in \bar{G}_{\Omega^k}\} \text{ for each } P \in S,$$

where $\bar{G}_{\Omega^k}$ is the closure of G_{Ω^k} and $G_{\Omega^k} = \{(P,y^k) \mid y^k \in \Omega^k(P),\ P \in S^{\sqcap},\ y^k \in A^k\}$.

Then η^k is the following mapping which associates the set $\eta^k(P)$ in A^k with each $P \in S$:

$$\text{(10.vi)} \qquad P \rightarrow \eta^k(P) : S \rightarrow A^k, \quad k=1,2, \ldots, \mu.$$

Obviously, this mapping η^k is closed. If the image $\eta^k(P)$ is not convex, we define

---

96. See Berge [1] p. 113 and Nikaido [17] p. 314.
97. Cf. Nikaido [17] p. 317 for the condition of extension of mappings.

$\bar{\eta}^k(P)$ by (10.vii) :

$$(10.\text{vii}) \qquad \bar{\eta}^k(P) = \{y^k \mid y^k \in C(\eta^k(P)),\ y^k \in A^k\} \text{ for each } P \in S :$$

where $C(\eta^k(P))$ is the convex hull of $\eta^k(P)$.

Now,

$$(10.\text{viii}) \qquad P \to \bar{\eta}^k(P) : S \to A^k, \quad k=1,2, \ldots, \mu.$$

That is, $\bar{\eta}^k$ is the mapping which associates the convex hull of $\eta^k(P)$ in A^k with each $P \in S$; moreover, this mapping $\bar{\eta}^k$ is closed.[98] If we take the vectorial sum of these closed mappings $\bar{\eta}^k$:

$$(10.\text{ix}) \qquad P \to \Lambda(P) = \sum_{k=1}^{\mu} \bar{\eta}^k(P) : S \to A = \sum_{k=1}^{\mu} A^k, \quad k=1,2, \ldots, \mu.$$

We see that the mapping Λ is closed and its image $\Lambda(P)$ is convex.[99]

Here we will explain some topological properties of the maximum value of $\Pi_{o,k}$. Then, we will explain some topological properties of ${}^m\pi_{o,k}(P)$ and ${}^m\pi^k_{t,k}(P)$ defined below. We let ${}^m\Pi_{o,k}(P)$ denote the maximum value of $\Pi_{o,k}$ for each $P \in \bar{S}^{¤}$. Obviously, this value is non-negative.[100] If we consider the following mapping which associates ${}^m\Pi_{o,k}(P)$ in R^1_+ with each $P \in S^{¤}$:

$$(10.\text{x}) \qquad P \to {}^m\Pi_{o,k}(P) : S^{¤} \to R^1_+, \quad k=1,2, \ldots, \mu.$$

then ${}^m\Pi_{o,k}$ is single-valued and continuous.[101]

Let ${}^m\pi_{o,k}(P)$ and ${}^m\pi^k_{t,k}(P)$ $(t=1,2, \ldots, \tau)$ denote the k-th firm's profit of the 0-th or t-th period, respectively, in the case where the firm maximizes the present value $\Pi_{o,k}$ for each $P \in S^{¤}$.

---

98. See Nikaido [17] pp. 317-318.
99. See Nikaido [17] p. 315 and pp. 197-198.
100. It is non-negative because $y^k=0$ is a feasible solution.
101. See Berge, *op.cit.* pp. 115-117 or Haga and Otsuki, *op.cit.* pp. 122-123.

a) $^{m}\pi_{o,k}(P)$ and $^{m}\pi^{k}_{t,k}(P)(t=1,2, \ldots, \tau)$ are non-negative.

The non-negativity of $^{m}\pi^{k}_{\tau,k}(P)$ comes from (3.d). The non-negativity of $^{m}\pi_{o,k}(P)$ and $^{m}\pi^{k}_{t,k}(P)(t=1,2, \ldots, \tau-1)$ can be easily verified. For example, suppose that $^{m}\pi_{o,k}(P)$ and $^{m}\pi^{k}_{3,k}(P)$ are negative by employing y^{k}, then we can choose another vector, $y^{k^{\alpha}}$, which belongs to A^{k} and satisfies (3)',(3.a)',(3.c), and (3.d) such that $^{m}\pi_{o,k}(P)$ and $^{m}\pi^{k}_{3,k}(P)$ become non-negative. We see that such a $y^{k^{\alpha}}$ is as follows :

(i) $y^{k^{\alpha}}_{o}$ and $y^{k^{\alpha}}_{3}$ are both zero vectors.

(ii) $y^{k^{\alpha}}_{t}$ $(t\neq 0, t\neq 3)$ is the same as y^{k}_{t} $(t\neq 0, t\neq 3)$, *i.e.*,

$$y^{k^{\alpha}}_{t} = y^{k}_{t} \quad (t\neq 0, t\neq 3).$$

(iii) $y^{k^{\alpha}}_{t,n+1} = y^{k}_{t,n+1}$ $(t=0,1, \ldots, \tau-1)$, and

$$y^{k^{\alpha}}_{t,o} = y^{k}_{t,o} \quad (t=0,1, \ldots, \tau-1).$$

It is clear that $y^{k^{\alpha}}_{t}$ belonging to A^{k} satisfies (3)',(3.b),(3.c), and (3.d).

Moreover, it can be verified from Assumptions IV.4 and IV.8 that $y^{k^{\alpha}}$ satisfies (3.a)' as well. In the case where $\bar{y}^{k}_{o,j} + y^{k}_{o,j} \geqq 0$ $(j \in \tilde{I}^{k})$, the proof is simple. However, in the case where $\bar{y}^{k}_{o,j} + y^{k}_{o,j} < 0$ for some $j \in \tilde{I}^{k}$ and $\bar{y}^{k}_{o,j} + y^{k}_{o,j} \geqq 0$ for the remaining $j \in \tilde{I}^{k}$, the proof that $y^{k^{\alpha}}$ satisfies (3.a)' requires additional attention. Now, let us define the new notation $\tilde{I}'^{k}$ and $\tilde{I}''^{k}$ as follows: $\tilde{I}'^{k} = \{j | j \in \tilde{I}^{k}$ and $\bar{y}^{k}_{o,j} + y^{k}_{o,j} < 0\}$, and $\tilde{I}''^{k} = \{j | j \in \tilde{I}^{k}$ and $\bar{y}^{k}_{o,j} + y^{k}_{o,j} \geqq 0\}$. And we note the fact that in the 0-th period $\{-(\sum_{j\in I^{k}} P_{o,j}\kappa^{k}_{o,j}y^{k}_{o,j} + \sum_{j\in \tilde{I}'^{k}} P_{o,j}\kappa^{k}_{o,j}y^{k}_{o,j} + \sum_{j\in \tilde{I}''^{k}} P_{o,j}\kappa^{k}_{o,j}y^{k}_{o,j})$

$+ \sum_{j\in\tilde{I}'^k} P_{o,j}\kappa^k_{o,j}y^k_{o,j} - \sum_{j\in\tilde{I}'^k} P_{o,j}y^k_{o,j} + \sum_{j\in\tilde{I}'^k} P_{o,j}\kappa^k_{o,j}\bar{y}^k_{o,j} - \sum_{j\in\tilde{I}'^k} P_{o,j}\bar{y}^k_{o,j}\}$ is positive[102]

because $(- \sum_{j\in I^k} P_{o,j}\kappa^k_{o,j}y^k_{o,j} - \sum_{j\in\tilde{I}'^k} P_{o,j}\kappa^k_{o,j}y^k_{o,j} - \sum_{j\in\tilde{I}''^k} P_{o,j}\kappa^k_{o,j}y^k_{o,j})$ is positive due to Assumptions IV.4, IV.8 and the supposition of the negativity of ${}^m\pi_{o,k}$. Similarly, in the 3rd period $(- \sum_{j\in\tilde{I}^k} P_{o,j}y^k_{o,j} - \sum_{j\in I^k} P_{o,j}\kappa^k_{o,j}y^k_{o,j})$ is positive (Assumption IV.8 is not needed to show this). Therefore, we can see that y^{k^α} satisfies (3.a)'. That is, ${}^m\pi_{o,k}(P)$ and ${}^m\pi^k_{3,k}(P)$ become non-negative by employing y^{k^α}. This result contradicts the definition of ${}^m\Pi_{o,k}$. That is, our supposition of the negativity of ${}^m\pi_{o,k}$ and ${}^m\pi^k_{3,k}$ is wrong. Thus, ${}^m\pi_{o,k}(P)$ and ${}^m\pi^k_{t,k}(P)(t=1,2, \ldots, \tau-1)$ are non-negative.

(*Q.E.D.*)

b) ${}^m\pi_{o,k}(P)$ and ${}^m\pi^k_{t,k}(P)(t=1,2, \ldots, \tau)$ are single-valued for each $P \in S^\mu$.

It follows from the single-valuedness of Ω^k_* (for each $P \in S^\mu$) and the definitions of $\pi_{o,k}$ and $\pi^k_{t,k}(t=1,2, \ldots, \tau-1)$ that ${}^m\pi_{o,k}(P)$ and ${}^m\pi^k_{t,k}(P)(t=1,2, \ldots, \tau-1)$ are single-valued for each $P \in S^\mu$. Also, it follows from the fact that ${}^m\Pi_{\bar{o},k}(P)$, ${}^m\pi_{o,k}(P)$ and ${}^m\pi^k_{t,k}(P)(t=1,2, \ldots, \tau-1)$ are single-valued for each $P \in S^\mu$ that ${}^m\pi^k_{\tau,k}(P)$ is single-valued for each $P \in S^\mu$. (*Q.E.D.*)

---

102. This expression is derived as follows:
   (1) transpose all the terms concerning money and bonds to the left-hand side and the other terms to the right-hand side;
   (2) substitute the optimal y^k_o (in the case where ${}^m\pi_{o,k}(P)$ is negative by employing y^k_o) into the right-hand side in (1);
   (3) substitute $y^{k^\alpha}_o = 0$ for y^k_o of the right-hand side in (1);
   (4) subtract the right-hand side made in (2) from the right-hand side made in (3). This yields the expression of our text.

If we consider the following mappings :

$$(10.xi) \qquad P \to {}^m\pi_{o,k}(P) : S^{\alpha} \to R^1_+$$

$$P \to {}^m\pi^k_{t,k}(P) : S^{\alpha} \to R^1_+, \quad t=1,2, \ldots, \tau.$$

then from a) and b), and from the continuity of the mapping Ω^k_* and ${}^m\Pi_{o,k}$, we see that ${}^m\pi_{o,k}$ and ${}^m\pi^k_{t,k}$ are single-valued continuous functions and the images ${}^m\pi_{o,k}(P)$ and ${}^m\pi^k_{t,k}(P)$ are non-negative for each k. Therefore, these properties are completely consistent with Assumption VI.3.

2.1.2. Modified *ex ante* Demand or Supply Functions of Individual Households

Now we will define demand or supply functions of households by restricting the original choice sets of the utility maximization problem within B^i.

2.1.2. a. Demand or Supply Functions of Individual Labourers

In order to construct the i-th (i=1,2, ..., h) labourer's individual demand or supply function, first define $f^i(P)$ for every labourer i by (11.i) :

$$(11.i) \qquad f^i(P) = \{x^i \mid x^i = \text{maximizer of (1.i), subject to (2.i)'}, \text{(2.i.a)', (2.i.b), and } x^i \in B^i\} \text{ for each } P \in S^o.$$

Then consider the following mapping which associates the set $f^i(P)$ in B^i with $P \in S^o$:

$$(11.ii) \qquad P \to f^i(P) : S^o \to B^i, \quad i=1,2, \ldots, h.$$

We will show below that this mapping f^i (i=1,2, ..., h) is also closed, by a method analogous to the one employed in proving the closedness of Ω^k. That is, we will first show the continuity of the following mapping :

$$(11.iii) \qquad P \to f^i_f(P) : S^o \to B^i, \quad i=1,2, \ldots, h,$$

where $f^i_f(P)$ is the set of feasible solutions (which belong to B^i) of (2.i)', (2.i.a)', and (2.i.b) for each given $P \in S^o$.

The mapping $f_f^i(i=1,2, \ldots, h)$ is upper semi-continuous and lower semi-continuous on S^o.[103] Hence, this mapping is continuous on S^o. The utility function is a continuous numerical function (cf. Assumption I.3), and the image $f_f^i(P)$ for each $P \in S^o$ is non-empty. Consequently, by virtue of Berge's Maximum theorem, the mapping f^i of (11.ii) is closed.[104] (*Q.E.D.*) It is, in general, a multi-valued mapping.

Next, for each $x^i = (x_o^i, x_{o,n+1}^i, x_{o,o}^i, x_1^i, x_{1,n+1}^i, x_{1,o}^i, \ldots, x_\tau^i) \in f^i(P)$, let

$$x_*^i = (x_o^i, x_1^i, \ldots, x_\tau^i).$$

We will call this x_*^i the subvector of x^i, as stated above for y_*^k.

Now, let

$$f_*^i(P) = \{x_*^i \mid x^i \in f^i(P),\ x_*^i \in B_*^i\} \text{ for each } P \in S^o,$$

$$\text{where } B_*^i = B_o^i \times B_1^i \times B_2^i \times \ldots \times B_\tau^i.$$

Then f_*^i can be considered to be the following mapping which associates the set $f_*^i(P)$ in B_*^i with each $P \in S^o$:

$$\text{(11.iv)} \qquad P \to f_*^i(P) : S^o \to B_*^i, \quad i=1,2, \ldots, h.$$

This mapping f_*^i is single-valued and continuous.[105] The single-valuedness of f_*^i can be shown by a method similar to the one employed in showing the single-

---

103. See pp. 58-59 above, or see Berge, *op.cit.*, pp. 111-112, Haga and Otsuki [10] pp. 122-123, and footnote 89 on p. 59 above, for the upper semi-continuity of f_f^i. The other property of continuity, that is, the lower semi-continuity of f_f^i, is derived from the existence of a vector x^i which belongs to B^i and satisfied the inequalities (2.i)' and (2.i.a)' in strict inequality, as well as the inequalities (2.i.b) not necessarily in strict inequality (cf. p. 59 above). For a fuller explanation, see Appendix II.

104. See "Maximum theorem" in Berge, *op.cit.*, pp. 115-117 or Haga and Otsuki *op.cit.*, pp. 122-123. (Cf. pp. 58-59 above.)

105. f_*^i is concerned with only real goods other than bonds and money stock, as is Ω_*^k.

valuedness of Ω^k_*. That is, if f^i_* is not single-valued, then there exist two different vectors $x^{i^1}_*$ and $x^{i^2}_*$, where $x^{i^1}_* \in f^i_*(P)$ and $x^{i^2}_* \in f^i_*(P)$.

By definition of x^i_* and x^i, there exist two different maximum solutions x^{i^1} and x^{i^2} which have $x^{i^1}_*$ and $x^{i^2}_*$ as their subvectors, respectively. Now construct the following convex linear combination :

$$(\alpha.\text{i}) \qquad x^i(\lambda) = \lambda x^{i^1} + (1-\lambda)x^{i^2}, \text{ where } 0 < \lambda < 1.$$

This $x^i(\lambda)$ satisfies the non-linear inequalities (2.i.a)' as well as the linear inequalities (2.i)' and (2.i.b).[106] Needless to say, $x^i(\lambda) \in B^i$. Next, corresponding to (α.i), the following convex combination is directly derived from the definition of x^i_*.

$$(\alpha.\text{ii}) \qquad x^i_*(\lambda) = \lambda x^{i^1}_* + (1-\lambda)x^{i^2}_*, \text{ where } 0 < \lambda < 1.$$

It follows from Assumption I.4 that $u^i(x^i_*(\lambda)) > u^i(x^{i^1}_*) = u^i(x^{i^2}_*)$. This contradicts the optimality of x^{i^1} (or x^{i^2}) whose subvector is $x^{i^1}_*$ (or $x^{i^2}_*$). Thus, the mapping $f^i_*(i=1,2, \ldots, h)$ is single-valued. The continuity of f^i_* is easily shown by virtue of the upper semi-continuity of f^i.[107] *(Q.E.D.)*

Now, let the closed mapping f^i extend to a closed mapping ψ^i from $S(\supset S^o)$ into B^i.[108] Define $\psi^i(P)$ by (11.v) :

$$(11.\text{v}) \qquad \psi^i(P) = \{x^i \mid x^i \in B^i, (P,x^i) \in \bar{G}_{f^i} \text{ for each } P \in S,$$

where $\bar{G}_{f^i}$ is the closure of G_{f^i} and $G_{f^i} = \{(P,x^i) \mid x^i \in f^i(P), P \in S^o, x^i \in B^i\}$.

106. It is verified, by making use of Appendix III, that $x^i(\lambda)$ satisfies the non-linear inequalities (2.i.a)'. See Appendix III on pp. 110-111 below. (Cf. p. 60 above.)
107. See p. 61.
108. Cf. footnote 97 on p. 61 above.

Then ψ^i is the following mapping which associates the set $\psi^i(P)$ in B^i with each $P \in S$:

$$(11.vi) \qquad P \to \psi^i(P) : S \to B^i, \quad i=1,2, \ldots, h.$$

Obviously, this mapping ψ^i is closed. If the image $\psi^i(P)$ is not convex, we define $\bar{\psi}^i(P)$ by (11.vii) :

$$(11.vii) \qquad \bar{\psi}^i(P) = \{x^i \mid x^i \in C(\psi^i(P)), x^i \in B^i\} \text{ for each } P \in S,$$

where $C(\psi^i(P))$ is the convex hull of $\psi^i(P)$.

Now,

$$(11.viii) \qquad P \to \bar{\psi}^i(P) : S \to B^i, \quad i=1,2, \ldots, h.$$

That is, $\bar{\psi}^i$ is the mapping which associates the convex hull of $\psi^i(P)$ in B^i with each $P \in S$, moreover, this mapping $\bar{\psi}^i$ is closed.[109]

2.1.2. b. Demand or Supply Functions of Individual Rentiers

We will construct demand or supply functions of the i-th rentier ($i=h+1,h+2, \ldots, \ell$), but we must use for rentiers a procedure different from that employed for firms and labourers in order to accomplish our existence proof. Above, the mappings Ω^k and f^i were respectively defined for each $P \in S^{\sqcap}$ only and each $P \in S^o$ only, and they were extended to closed mappings η^k and ψ^i. For rentiers, we must construct the mapping on a new domain $S^* \times \Xi$ and then we will extend it to a closed mapping from $S \times \Xi$ ($\supset S^* \times \Xi$) into B^i.[110]

Now, let Ξ denote the Cartesian product $A^1 \times A^2 \times \ldots \times A^\mu$, where $\Xi \ni (y^1, y^2, \ldots, y^\mu)$. Next, construct the new set S^* for rentiers as follows.[111]

a) If all of the i-th rentier's $\kappa^i_{t,n+1}$'s($t=0,1, \ldots, \tau-1$) are positive, and if he has some good q, other than bonds or money

109. Cf. footnote 98 on p. 62 above.
110. Cf. the i-th rentier's budget constraints (2.ii)" on p. 35.
111. Cf. p. 58 and p. 39 above for the difference between S^* and $S^{\sqcap}$ or S^o.

stock, as his initial holding in the 0-th period, then S^* is defined for such a rentier by (12.i) :[112]

(12.i) $S^* = S_o \times S_n^*$ where $S_n^* = \{(P_{o,2}, P_{o,3}, \ldots, P_{o,n+1}, \bar{z}) \mid P_{o,q} + P_{o,n+1} > 0,\ P_{o,j} \geqq 0\ (j=2,3, \ldots, n+1)$, and $\sum_{j=2}^{n+1} P_{o,j} + \bar{z} = 1\}$.

b) If all of the i-th rentier's $\kappa_{t,n+1}^{i}$'s$(t=0,1, \ldots, \tau-1)$ are positive and if he has money stock but no real goods as his initial holdings in the 0-th period, then S^* is defined for such a rentier by (12.ii):

(12.ii) $S^* = S_o \times S_n^*$ where $S_n^* = \{(P_{o,2}, P_{o,3}, \ldots, P_{o,n+1}, \bar{z}) \mid P_{o,n+1} + \bar{z} > 0,\ P_{o,j} \geqq 0\ (j=2,3, \ldots, n+1)$, and $\sum_{j=2}^{n+1} P_{o,j} + \bar{z} = 1\}$.

c) If all of the i-th rentier's $\kappa_{t,n+1}^{i}$'s$(t=0,1, \ldots, \tau-1)$ are not positive, and if he has some good q, other than bond or money stock, as his initial holding in the 0-th period, then S^* is defined for such a rentier by (12.iii):

(12.iii) $S^* = S_o \times S_n^*$ where $S_n^* = \{(P_{o,2}, P_{o,3}, \ldots, P_{o,n+1}, \bar{z}) \mid P_{o,q} > 0,\ P_{o,j} \geqq 0\ (j=2,3, \ldots, n+1: j \neq q),\ \bar{z} \geqq 0$ and $\sum_{j=2}^{n+1} P_{o,j} + \bar{z} = 1\}$.

d) If all of the i-th rentier's $\kappa_{t,n+1}^{i}$'s$(t=0,1, \ldots, \tau-1)$ are not positive, and if he has money stock but no real goods as

112. In cases of a) and c), such a rentier may or may not have bonds or money stock.

his initial holdings in the 0-th period, then S^* is defined for such a rentier by (12.iv):

(12.iv) $S^* = S_o \times S_n^*$ where $S_n^* = \{(P_{o,2}, P_{o,3}, \ldots, P_{o,n+1}, \bar{z}) \mid \bar{z} > 0,$

$P_{o,j} \geqq 0$ (j=2,3, ..., n+1), and $\sum_{j=2}^{n+1} P_{o,j} + \bar{z} = 1\}$.

From the above definitions of S^*, we can associate every rentier with one, and only one, appropriate set of S^*'s, from (12.i) to (12.iv).[113] Accordingly, if we form the Cartesian product $S^* \times \Xi$ such that $(P, y^1, y^2, \ldots, y^\mu) \in S^* \times \Xi$, then we can define every rentier's demand or supply function on this $S^* \times \Xi$ as follows.

---

113. We employ the set S^* merely as a device to construct the demand or supply functions of households and firms. For the construction of these functions, we must know what will be the quantity demanded or supplied by each individual household and firm at each one of all combinations of the various hypothetical prices and money stocks. We must know what will be the quantity demanded or supplied at every possible quantity or value (including zero) of money stock, as well as of real assets, in the budget constraints and money constraints. Thus S^* is adopted only as a technical procedure in constructing the demand or supply functions.

Each S^* in (12.i),(12.ii), and (12.iii) contains a vector $P = (P_{o,1}, P_{o,2}, \ldots, P_{o,n+1}, \bar{z})$ with $\bar{z} = 0$. But if an element $\bar{z}$ of vector $P \in S^*$ happens to be zero in constructing these functions, it means only that households and firms do not have their own cash balances at the beginning of the period, though they may have real assets of some value. That is, if an element $\bar{z}$ (not $\bar{Z}_o$) of P is zero, it should not be supposed that the money, as the general means of exchange, disappears from the whole economic system and that the money system is abolished.

But in the case where $\bar{Z}_o = 0$, the function W will need a different interpretation from the one stated above (cf. $\bar{w} = W(P_{o,2}, P_{o,3}, \ldots, P_{o,n+1}, \bar{Z}_o)$ in Assumption VII a) p. 29). Take any point $(P_{o,2}, P_{o,3}, \ldots, P_{o,n+1}, \bar{Z}_o) \in R_+^{n+1}$ where $\bar{Z}_o$ is zero and choose any sequence of points $\{(P_{o,2}^\nu, P_{o,3}^\nu, \ldots, P_{o,n+1}^\nu, \bar{Z}_o^\nu)\}$, $((P_{o,2}^\nu, P_{o,3}^\nu, \ldots, P_{o,n+1}^\nu, \bar{Z}_o^\nu) \in R_+^{n+1})$, that converges to the point $(P_{o,2}, P_{o,3}, \ldots, P_{o,n+1}, 0)$ in the domain R_+^{n+1} of the function W. That is, $\lim_{\nu \to \infty} (P_{o,2}^\nu, P_{o,3}^\nu, \ldots, P_{o,n+1}^\nu, \bar{Z}_o^\nu) = (P_{o,2}, P_{o,3}, \ldots, P_{o,n+1}, 0)$. We assume that the image $\{W(P_{o,2}^\nu, P_{o,3}^\nu, \ldots, P_{o,n+1}^\nu, \bar{Z}_o^\nu)\}$ converges, *i.e.* that the limit of $\{W(P_{o,2}^\nu, P_{o,3}^\nu, \ldots, P_{o,n+1}^\nu, \bar{Z}_o^\nu)\}$ exists. Also, we define the image $W(P_{o,2}, P_{o,3}, \ldots, P_{o,n+1}, 0)$ by the limit of $\{W(P_{o,2}^\nu, P_{o,3}^\nu, \ldots, P_{o,n+1}^\nu, \bar{Z}_o^\nu)\}$. The function W in Assumption VII is, in fact, defined in this way. In the

Define $\psi^i(P,y^1,y^2, \ldots, y^\mu)$ by (12.v):

$$\text{(12.v)} \quad \psi^i(P,y^1,y^2, \ldots, y^\mu) = \{ x^i \mid x^i = \text{maximizer of (1.ii),}$$
$$\text{subject to (2.ii)'', (2.ii.a)', (2.ii.b), and } x^i \in B^i\}$$
$$\text{for each } (P,y^1,y^2, \ldots, y^\mu) \in S^* \times \Xi.$$

Consider the mapping ψ^i which associates the set $\psi^i(P,y^1,y^2, \ldots, y^\mu)$ in B^i with each $(P,y^1,y^2, \ldots, y^\mu) \in S^* \times \Xi$:[114]

$$\text{(12.vi)} \quad (P,y^1,y^2, \ldots, y^\mu) \to \psi^i(P,y^1,y^2, \ldots, y^\mu):$$
$$S^* \times \Xi \to B^i, \quad i=h+1,h+2, \ldots, \ell.$$

We will prove below that this mapping ψ^i is also closed, but only the essence of the proof will be given, since a similar proof has already been given in (10.ii) and (11.ii).

In order to verify that the mapping is closed, we have only to show the continuity of the following mapping:

$$\text{(12.vii)} \quad (P,y^1,y^2, \ldots, y^\mu) \to \psi^i_f(P,y^1,y^2, \ldots, y^\mu):$$
$$S^* \times \Xi \to B^i, \quad i=h+1,h+2, \ldots, \ell,$$

where $\psi^i_f(P,y^1,y^2, \ldots, y^\mu)$ is the set of feasible solutions (which belong to B^i) of (2.ii)'',(2.ii.a)', and (2.ii.b) for each $(P,y^1,y^2, \ldots, y^\mu) \in S^* \times \Xi$. As in (10.iii) and (11.iii), the mapping ψ^i_f is continuous on $S^* \times \Xi$.[115]

---

last stage of our existence proof, we will demonstrate that an element $\bar{z}$ of the normalized vector of $(P_{o,2},P_{o,3}, \ldots, P_{o,n+1},\bar{Z}_o)$ is not zero in an equilibrium.

114. As will be easily seen, what is actually related to (2.ii)'' is not y^k but a subvector y^k_o of y^k.

115. Since the upper semi-continuity of ψ^i_f can be easily verified, we have only to verify the lower semi-continuity of ψ^i_f. This is derived from the existence of a vector x^i which belongs to B^i and satisfies the inequalities (2.ii)'' and

Moreover, the utility function (1.ii) is a continuous numerical function (cf. Assumption I.3) and the image $\psi^i_f(P,y^1,y^2, \ldots, y^\mu)$ for each $(P,y^1,y^2, \ldots, y^\mu) \in S^* \times \Xi$ is non-empty. Accordingly, by virtue of Berge's Maximum theorem, the mapping ψ^i of (12.vi) is closed.[116] (*Q.E.D.*)

Now, let the closed mapping ψ^i extend to a closed mapping ζ from $S \times \Xi$ into B^i.[117] First, define $\zeta^i(P,y^1,y^2, \ldots, y^\mu)$ by (12.viii):

(12.viii) $\zeta^i(P,y^1,y^2, \ldots, y^\mu) = \{x^i \mid x^i \in B^i, (P,y^1,y^2, \ldots, y^\mu,x^i) \in \bar{G}_{\psi^i}\}$ for each $(P,y^1,y^2, \ldots, y^\mu) \in S \times \Xi$,

where $\bar{G}_{\psi^i}$ is the closure of G_{ψ^i} and $G_{\psi^i} = \{(P,y^1,y^2, \ldots, y^\mu,x^i) \mid x^i \in \psi^i(P,y^1,y^2, \ldots, y^\mu),$ $(P,y^1,y^2, \ldots, y^\mu) \in S^* \times \Xi, x^i \in B^i\}$.

Then, ζ^i is the following mapping which associates the set $\zeta^i(P,y^1,y^2, \ldots, y^\mu)$ in B^i with each $(P,y^1,y^2, \ldots, y^\mu) \in S \times \Xi$:

(12.ix) $(P,y^1,y^2, \ldots, y^\mu) \to \zeta^i(P,y^1,y^2, \ldots, y^\mu)$:

$S \times \Xi \to B^i$, $i=h+1,h+2, \ldots, \ell$.

Obviously, this mapping ζ^i is closed. If the image $\zeta^i(P,y^1,y^2, \ldots, y^\mu)$ is not convex, we define $\bar{\zeta}^i(P,y^1,y^2, \ldots, y^\mu)$ by (12.x):

(12.x) $\bar{\zeta}^i(P,y^1,y^2, \ldots, y^\mu) = \{x^i \mid x^i \in C(\zeta^i(P,y^1,y^2, \ldots, y^\mu)),$ $x^i \in B^i\}$ for each $(P,y^1,y^2, \ldots, y^\mu) \in S \times \Xi$,

where $C(\zeta^i(P,y^1,y^2, \ldots, y^\mu))$ is the

(2.ii.a)' in strict inequality, as well as the inequality (2.ii.b) not necessarily in strict inequality. Of course, the above x^i must satisfy the last equality of (2.ii)", *i.e.*, $x^i_{t,1} = 0$ $(t=0,1, \ldots, \tau)$. The existence of such a x^i can be relatively easily verified. A complete verification of the most difficult case will be made in Appendix II.

116. See footnote 91 on p. 59 above.

117. See footnote 97 on p. 61 above.

convex hull of $\zeta^i(P,y^1,y^2, \ldots, y^\mu)$.

Consider the following mapping $\bar{\zeta}^i$ which associates the convex hull of $\zeta^i(P,y^1,y^2, \ldots, y^\mu)$ in B^i with each $(P,y^1,y^2, \ldots, y^\mu) \in S \times \Xi$:

$$\text{(12.xi)} \qquad (P,y^1,y^2, \ldots, y^\mu) \to \bar{\zeta}^i(P,y^1,y^2, \ldots, y^\mu): \\ S \times \Xi \to B^i, \quad i=h+1,h+2, \ldots, \ell.$$

Obviously, this mapping $\bar{\zeta}^i$ is closed and the image $\bar{\zeta}^i(P,y^1,y^2, \ldots, y^\mu)$ is convex.[118]

2.2 Modified Individual Demand or Supply Functions based on the Dual-Decision Hypothesis

Now we will construct demand or supply functions of labourers based on the dual-decision hypothesis, but still we will construct them by restricting the original choice sets of the utility maximization problem within B^i.

2.2.1 Modified Demand or Supply Functions of Individual Labourers based on the Dual-Decision Hypothesis

For each $x_o^i = (x_{o,1}^i, x_{o,2}^i, \ldots, x_{o,n}^i)$ which is a subvector of x_*^i, where $x_*^i = (x_o^i, x_1^i, \ldots, x_T^i) = f_*^i(P)$ for each $P \in S^o$, consider $x_{o,1}^i$. Let

$$\text{(13.i)} \qquad f_{o,1}^i(P) \doteq \{x_{o,1}^i \mid x_*^i = f_*^i(P),\ x_{o,1}^i \in D_{o,1}^i\} \\ \text{for each } P \in S^o.$$[119]

If we consider the following mapping which associates the set $f_{o,1}^i(P)$ in $D_{o,1}^i$ with each $P \in S^o$,

$$\text{(13.ii)} \qquad P \to f_{o,1}^i(P) : S^o \to D_{o,1}^i, \quad i=1,2, \ldots, h,$$

---

118. Cf. footnote 98 on p. 62 above.

119. $D_{o,1}^i$ is the set $D_{o,1}^i = \{x_{o,1}^i \mid x_{o,1}^i = b_{o,1}^i + x_{o,1}^i \;;\; x_{o,1}^i \geqq 0\}$ where $b_{o,1}^i$ means the infimum of labour in the 0-th period of the i-th labourer. (Cf.

then $f^i_{o,1}$ is single-valued and continuous. This is clear because f^i_* is single-valued and continuous.

Let $\Sigma_S(P)$ denote $\sum_{i=1}^{h} f^i_{o,1}(P)$. That is, $\Sigma_S(P)$ is the total supply of labour in the whole system in the 0-th period for each $P \in S^o$. Consider the following mapping $\Sigma_S(P)$ which associates the point $\Sigma_S(P)$ in $D^*_{o,1}$ with each $P \in S^o$:[120]

$$\text{(13.iii)} \qquad P \to \Sigma_S(P) : S^o \to D^*_{o,1}.$$

Obviously, the mapping $\Sigma_S(P)$ is single-valued and continuous.

For each $y^k_o = (y^k_{o,1}, y^k_{o,2}, \ldots, y^k_{o,n})$ of the subvector of each y^k_*, where $y^k_* = (y^k_o, y^k_1, \ldots, y^k_\tau) = \Omega^k_*(P)$ for each $P \in S^\pi$, consider $y^i_{o,1}$. Let

$$\text{(13.iv)} \qquad \Omega^k_{o,1}(P) = \{y^k_{o,1} \mid y^k_* = \Omega^k_*(P),\ y^k_{o,1} \in Q^k_{o,1}\}$$

$$\text{for each } P \in S^\pi.$$[121]

If we consider the following mapping which associates the set $\Omega^k_{o,1}(P)$ in $Q^k_{o,1}$ with each $P \in S^\pi$:

$$\text{(13.v)} \qquad P \to \Omega^k_{o,1}(P) : S^\pi \to Q^k_{o,1}, \quad k=1,2, \ldots, \mu,$$

then, $\Omega^k_{o,1}$ is single-valued and continuous. This is clear, because Ω^k_* is single-valued and continuous.

Let $\Sigma_D(P)$ denote $\sum_{k=1}^{\mu} \Omega^k_{o,1}(P)$. That is, $\Sigma_D(P)$ is the total demand for labour in the whole system in the 0-th period, for each $P \in S^\pi$.

Assumption I.1.)

120. $D^*_{o,1} = \sum_{i=1}^{h} D^i_{o,1}$ *i.e.*, $D^*_{o,1}$ is the vectorial sum of the sets $D^i_{o,1}$.

121. $Q^k_{o,1}$ is the set which consists of all elements $y^k_{o,1}$ of y^k_o $(\in Q^k_o)$.

Consider the following mapping which associates the point $\Sigma_D(P)$ in $Q^*_{o,1}$ with each $P \in S^\mu$:[122]

$$\text{(13.vi)} \qquad P \to \Sigma_D(P) \; : \; S^\mu \to Q^*_{o,1}.$$

Obviously, $\Sigma_D(P)$ is single-valued and continuous.

Next, we must consider the total labour supply in the 0-th period, which is to be derived on the basis of the dual-decision hypothesis (*i.e.*, Assumption X).

First, define F(P) by (13.vii):

$$\text{(13.vii)} \qquad F(P) = \{\sum_{i=1}^{h} x^i_{o,1} \mid \sum_{i=1}^{h} x^i_{o,1} = \max(\Sigma_D(P), \Sigma_S(P)),$$

$$\sum_{i=1}^{h} x^i_{o,1} \in D^*_{o,1}\}, \text{ for each } P \in S^o.$$

F(P) is the total supply of labour in the 0-th period for each $P \in S^o$, under the dual-decision hypothesis.[123] Thus

$$\text{(13.viii)} \qquad P \to F(P) \; : \; S^o \to D^*_{o,1}.$$

This mapping F is a single-valued continuous function.

Next, define the i-th labourer's individual labour supply for each $P \in S^o$, *i.e.*, $\xi^i(P)$ by, (13.ix). This (13.ix) follows from Assumption X:

$$\text{(13.ix)} \qquad \xi^i(P) = \{x^i_{o,1} \mid x^i_{o,1} = \frac{f^i_{o,1}(P)\; F(P)}{\Sigma_S(P)}, \; x^i_{o,1} \in D^i_{o,1}\},$$

$$\text{for each } P \in S^o, \quad i=1,2, \ldots, h.$$

Now, if $\Sigma_S(P)$ is zero, $f^i_{o,1}(P)$ is zero for every $i(i=1,2, \ldots, h)$. Then, let us define the value of $\xi^i(P)$ as zero in the case where $\Sigma_S(P)$ is zero.

---

122. $Q^*_{o,1} = \sum_{k=1}^{\mu} Q^k_{o,1}$.

123. Clearly, F(P) is non-positive for each $P \in S^o$, because $\Sigma_D(P)$ and $\Sigma_S(P)$ are non-positive by definition.

$$(13.x) \qquad P \to \xi^i(P) : S^o \to D^i_{o,1}, \quad i=1,2, \ldots, h.$$

This function ξ^i is single-valued and continuous, as will be easily verified.[124]

We can construct each labourer's demand or supply function based on the dual-decision hypothesis as follows. First, the i-th labourer's budget constraints (2.i)' must be replaced by the following (2.i)" which differs from (2.i)' by the addition of the equality $x^i_{o,1} = \xi^i(P)$.

$$
(2.i)'' \quad
\begin{aligned}
& P_o x^i_o + P_{o,n+1} x^i_{o,n+1} + x^i_{o,o} \leqq \lambda^i \bar{Z}_o + P_o \bar{x}^i_o \\
& P^i_1 x^i_1 + P^i_{1,n+1} x^i_{1,n+1} + x^i_{1,o} \leqq x^i_{o,n+1} + x^i_{o,o} \\
& \cdots\cdots\cdots\cdots\cdots\cdots\cdots\cdots\cdots\cdots \\
& P^i_\tau x^i_\tau \leqq x^i_{\tau-1,n+1} + x^i_{\tau-1,o} \\
& x^i_{o,1} = \xi^i(P) \\
& x^i_{t,1} \leqq 0, \quad t=0,1, \ldots, \tau; \quad i=1,2, \ldots, h.
\end{aligned}
$$

In order to define the new demand or supply function of each labourer, let us define an $\tilde{f}^i(P)$ by (11.i)', different from the $f^i(P)$ defined above. Let $\tilde{x}^i$ denote x^i after the i-th labourer's dual-decision:

$$(11.i)' \qquad \tilde{f}^i(P) = \{\tilde{x}^i \mid \tilde{x}^i = \text{maximizer of (1.i), subject to (2.i)'', (2.i.a)', (2.i.b), and } \tilde{x}^i \in B^i\}, \text{ for each } P \in S^o.$$

Consider the following mapping $\tilde{f}^i$ which associates the set $\tilde{f}^i(P)$ in B^i with each $P \in S^o$:

$$(11.ii)' \qquad P \to \tilde{f}^i(P) : S^o \to B^i, \quad i=1,2, \ldots, h.$$

---

124. Suppose that, if $\Sigma_S(\bar{P}) = 0$ for $\bar{P} \in S^o$, $\xi^i(\bar{P}) = 0$. Then, notice that there exists an appropriate neighbourhood of $\bar{P}$, $U(\bar{P})$, such that $\dfrac{f^i_{o,1}(P)\, F(P)}{\Sigma_S(P)} =$

We can prove that this mapping $\tilde{f}^i$ is also closed, as is f^i. We can demonstrate this by a method similar to the one employed in proving the closedness of f^i, even though (2.i)" is slightly different from (2.i)'.

Let $\tilde{f}^i_f(P)$ denote the set of feasible solutions (which belong to B^i) of (2.i)", (2.i.a)', and (2.i.b) for each given $P \in S^o$. Then, consider the following mapping:

$$\text{(11.iii)'} \qquad P \to \tilde{f}^i_f(P) : S^o \to B^i, \quad i=1,2, \ldots, h.$$

This mapping f^i_f is continuous.[125] We know that the utility function (1.i) is a continuous numerical function, and that the image $\tilde{f}^i_f(P)$ for each $P \in S^o$ is non-empty.

$f^i_{o,1}$ or $\left| \dfrac{f^i_{o,1}(P)\ F(P)}{\Sigma_S(P)} \right| < \left| f^i_{o,1} \right|$ for every $P \in U(\bar{P})$.

125. The upper semi-continuity of $\tilde{f}^i_f$ is clear. (Cf. footnote 89 on p. 59 above.) Also, the proof of the lower semi-continuity of f^i_f is, with the application of Haga and Otsuki's Theorem A 1, not difficult (cf. Haga and Otsuki, *op.cit.*, pp. 122-123). The reason why this theorem can be applied, despite the addition of the equality $x^i_{o,1} = \xi^i(P)$, is that the function ξ^i is single-valued and continuous for each $P \in S^o$. The procedure of our proof is as follows.

First, for each given $P \in S^o$, choose an x^i such that

(i) it belongs to B^i,

(ii) it satisfies the inequalities (2.1)" (excluding the equality $x^i_{o,1} = \xi^i(P)$) and (2.i.a)' in strict inequality,

(iii) it satisfies the inequalities (2.i.b) not necessarily in strict inequality, and

(iv) it satisfies the equality $x^i_{o,1} = \xi^i(P)$.

Second, apply Haga and Otsuki's Theorem A 1, taking into account that ξ^i is a single-valued continuous function for each $P \in S^o$, and that $x^i_{o,1}$ is the first element of the vector x^i.

Thus, the lower semi-continuity of $\tilde{f}^i_f$ is verified.

As can be seen from this proof, an essential step in proving the lower semi-continuity of $\tilde{f}^i_f$ is to find an x^i which satisfies the inequalities (2.i)" (excluding $x^i_{o,1} = \xi^i(P)$) and (2.i.a)' in strict inequality. Note that, in the case where the dual-decision is supposed, we must find such an x^i in a way different from the case where the dual-decision is not supposed. See Appendix II.

Thus, by virtue of Berge's Maximum theorem, the mapping $\tilde{f}^i$ of (11.ii)' is closed.[126]

(*Q.E.D.*)

This $\tilde{f}^i$ is, in general, a multi-valued mapping. But, for each $\tilde{x}^i = (\tilde{x}^i_o, \tilde{x}^i_{o,n+1}, \tilde{x}^i_{o,o}, \tilde{x}^i_1, \tilde{x}^i_{1,n+1}, \tilde{x}^i_{1,o}, \ldots, \tilde{x}^i_T) \in \tilde{f}^i(P)$, let $\tilde{x}^i_* = (\tilde{x}^i_o, \tilde{x}^i_1, \ldots, \tilde{x}^i_T)$. Next, let

$$\tilde{f}^i_*(P) = \{\tilde{x}^i_* \mid \tilde{x}^i \in \tilde{f}^i(P),\ \tilde{x}^i_* \in B^i_*\} \text{ for each } P \in S^o.$$

Then, we consider the following mapping:

$$\text{(11.iv)'} \quad P \to \tilde{f}^i_*(P) : S^o \to B^i_*, \quad i=1,2, \ldots, h.$$

The mapping $\tilde{f}^i_*$ is single-valued and continuous.[127]

Now, let us extend the closed mapping $\tilde{f}^i$ to a closed mapping g^i from S into B^i. First, define $g(P)$ by (11.v)':

$$\text{(11.v)'} \quad g^i(P) = \{\tilde{x}^i \mid \tilde{x}^i \in B^i,\ (P, \tilde{x}^i) \in \bar{G}_{\tilde{f}^i}\} \text{ for each}$$

$P \in S$, where $\bar{G}_{\tilde{f}^i}$ is the closure of $G_{\tilde{f}^i}$ and $G_{\tilde{f}^i} = \{(P, \tilde{x}^i) \mid \tilde{x}^i \in \tilde{f}^i(P),\ P \in S^o,\ \tilde{x}^i \in B^i\}$.

If we consider the following mapping:

$$\text{(11.vi)'} \quad P \to g^i(P) : S \to B^i, \quad i=1,2, \ldots, h,$$

then, the mapping g^i extended from S into B^i is closed. If the image $g^i(P)$ is not convex, we define $\bar{g}^i(P)$ by (11.vii)':

$$\text{(11.vii)'} \quad \bar{g}^i(P) = \{\tilde{x}^i \mid \tilde{x}^i \in C(g^i(P)),\ \tilde{x}^i \in B^i\} \text{ for each}$$

$P \in S$, where $C(g^i(P))$ is the convex hull of $g^i(P)$.

Then,

$$\text{(11.viii)'} \quad P \to \bar{g}^i(P) : S \to B^i, \quad i=1,2, \ldots, h.$$

This mapping $\bar{g}^i$ is closed.[128]

---

126. Cf. footnote 91 on p. 59 above.
127. See pp. 66-67 above. Also, see pp. 60-61.
128. Cf. footnote 98 on p. 62 above.

3. The Existence Proof (1)

— The Model with Modified Functions based on the Dual-Decision Hypothesis —

As a necessary step in our existence proof, we must first form, on the basis of mappings (11.viii)' and (12.xi), the households' total demand or supply function of goods, including labour, bonds, and money stock.

3.1 Notation

X : X denotes $\sum_{i=1}^{h} x^i + \sum_{i=h+1}^{\ell} x^i$.

$\tilde{X}$: $\tilde{X}$ denotes X where each labourer acts according to the dual-decision hypothesis. That is, $\tilde{X} = \sum_{i=1}^{h} \tilde{x}^i + \sum_{i=h+1}^{\ell} x^i$.

$X_{o,j}$: $X_{o,j}$ is the total demand for (or total supply of) the j-th good (including labour, bonds and money stock) in the 0-th period. That is, $X_{o,1} (\leqq 0)$ represents the total labour supply, $X_{o,n+1}$ represents the total demand for (or the total supply of) bonds in the 0-th period, and $X_{o,o} (\geqq 0)$ represents the total demand for money stock in the 0-th period.

$\tilde{X}_{o,j}$: $\tilde{X}_{o,j}$ denotes $X_{o,j}$ where each labourer acts according to the dual-decision hypothesis.

B : $B = \sum_{i=1}^{\ell} B^i$.

3.2 The Existence Proof (1)

In constructing the households' total demand or supply function, first define $\Gamma(P, y^1, y^2, \ldots, y^\mu)$ by (14.i):

$$(14.\text{i}) \qquad \sum_{i=1}^{h} \bar{g}^i(P) + \sum_{i=h+1}^{\ell} \bar{\psi}^i(P, y^1, y^2, \ldots, y^\mu) = \Gamma(P, y^1, y^2, \ldots, y^\mu)$$

$$= \{\tilde{X} \mid \tilde{X} = \sum_{i=1}^{h} \tilde{x}^i + \sum_{i=h+1}^{\ell} x^i,\ \tilde{x}^i \in \bar{g}^i(P),\ x^i \in \bar{\psi}^i(P, y^1, y^2,$$

$\ldots, y^{\mu}), \tilde{X} \in B, \tilde{x}^{i} \in B^{i}(i=1,2, \ldots, h)$ and $x^{i} \in B^{i}(i=h+1, h+2, \ldots, \ell)\}$ for each $(P, y^{1}, y^{2}, \ldots, y^{\mu}) \in S \times \Xi$.

Next, consider the following mapping Γ which associates the set $\Gamma(P, y^{1}, y^{2}, \ldots, y^{\mu})$ in B with each $(P, y^{1}, y^{2}, \ldots, y^{\mu}) \in S \times \Xi$.

$$(14.ii) \qquad (P, y^{1}, y^{2}, \ldots, y^{\mu}) \to \Gamma(P, y^{1}, y^{2}, \ldots, y^{\mu}): S \times \Xi \to B.$$

This mapping Γ is closed and its image $\Gamma(P, y^{1}, y^{2}, \ldots, y^{\mu})$ is convex.[129] Also, B is a convex and compact set.[130]

Now that we have taken the preliminary step of constructing the mappings,let us go on to the existence proof.

Form the Cartesian product $H = S \times B \times A^{1} \times A^{2} \times \ldots \times A^{\mu}$. Obviously, H is a convex and compact set.[131] Then, define $J(P, X, y^{1}, y^{2}, \ldots, y^{\mu})$ by (15.i).[132]

$$(15.i) \qquad J(P, X, y^{1}, y^{2}, \ldots, y^{\mu}) = [P|\{P_{o,1} = \text{med}(\bar{w}, P_{o,1} + (X_{o,1} - \sum_{k=1}^{\mu} y^{k}_{o,1}), \hat{w})\}, \{P_{o,j} = \frac{1}{\theta} \max(0, P_{o,j} + \nu(X_{o,j} - \sum_{k=1}^{\mu} y^{k}_{o,j} - \sum_{i=1}^{\ell} \bar{x}^{i}_{o,j} - \sum_{k=1}^{\mu} \bar{y}^{k}_{o,j})) : j=2,3, \ldots, n\},$$
$$\{P_{o,n+1} = \frac{1}{\theta} \max(0, P_{o,n+1} + \nu(X_{o,n+1} + \sum_{k=1}^{\mu} y^{k}_{o,n+1})\}, \{\bar{z} = \frac{1}{\theta} \max(0, \bar{z} + \nu(X_{o,o} + \sum_{k=1}^{\mu} y^{k}_{o,o} - \bar{z}))\}]$$

for each $(P, X, y^{1}, y^{2}, \ldots, y^{\mu}) \in H$,

where ν is a sufficiently small positive number ($\nu < 1$) such that

---

129. Cf. footnote 99 on p. 62 above.

130. This follows because the vectorial sum of all B^{i}'s$(i=1,2, \ldots, \ell)$ is convex and compact. (Cf. Nikaido, *op.cit.*, pp. 197-198.)

131. The convexity and the compactness of H is evident. (Cf. Nikaido, *op.cit.*, pp. 196-197.)

132. For example, med(f,g,h) = min(max(f,g), max(g,h), max(f,h)). See Glustoff, *op.cit.*, footnote 3 on p. 332. Also, note that notation ν differs from that in footnotes 83, 113 and Appendix.

$$\frac{1}{n+1} > \nu\,|(X_{o,j} - \sum_{k=1}^{\mu} y^{k}_{o,j} - \sum_{i=1}^{\ell} \bar{x}_{o,j} - \sum_{k=1}^{\mu} \bar{y}^{k}_{o,j})|,\ j=2,3,\ \ldots,\ n,$$

$$\frac{1}{n+1} > \nu\,|(X_{o,n+1} + \sum_{k=1}^{\mu} y^{k}_{o,n+1})|,\ \text{and}$$

$$\frac{1}{n+1} > \nu\,|(X_{o,o} + \sum_{k=1}^{\mu} y^{k}_{o,o} - \bar{z})|\ \text{for all}\ (P,X,y^1,y^2,\ \ldots,\ y^{\mu}) \in H:$$

and where θ is a positive number such that

$$\theta = \sum_{j=2}^{n} \max\{0, P_{o,j} + \nu(X_{o,j} - \sum_{k=1}^{\mu} y^{k}_{o,j} - \sum_{i=1}^{\ell} \bar{x}^{i}_{o,j} - \sum_{k=1}^{\mu} \bar{y}^{k}_{o,j})\}$$

$$+ \max\{0, P_{o,n+1} + \nu(X_{o,n+1} + \sum_{k=1}^{\mu} y^{k}_{o,n+1})\} + \max\{0, \bar{z} + \nu(X_{o,o}$$

$$+ \sum_{k=1}^{\mu} y^{k}_{o,o} - \bar{z})\}.$$

Also, remember that there exists Assumption VII.a) for the minimum money wage $\bar{w}$ in (15.i).

Now, for every P, where $P = (P_{o,1}, P_{o,2}, \ldots, P_{o,n+1}, \bar{z}) \in J(P,X,y^1,y^2,\ \ldots,\ y^{\mu})$ and $J(P,X,y^1,y^2,\ \ldots,\ y^{\mu})$ is defined for each $(P,X,y^1,y^2,\ \ldots,\ y^{\mu}) \in H$, the following inequalities (β) hold:

$$(\beta)\quad \begin{aligned} & 0 < \bar{w}' \leqq P_{o,1} \leqq \hat{w} \\ & 0 \leqq P_{o,j},\quad j=2,3,\ \ldots,\ n+1 \\ & 0 \leqq \bar{z} \\ & \sum_{j=2}^{n+1} P_{o,j} + \bar{z} = 1. \end{aligned}$$

Accordingly, every $P \in S = S_o \times S_n$, where $P_{o,1} \in S_o$ and $(P_{o,2}, P_{o,3}, \ldots, P_{o,n+1}, \bar{z}) \in S_n$. That is, the image $J(P,X,y^1,y^2,\ \ldots,\ y^{\mu})$ for each $(P,X,y^1,y^2,\ \ldots,\ y^{\mu}) \in H$ is the convex subset of S.

If we consider the following J:

$$\text{(15.ii)}\qquad (P,X,y^1,y^2,\ \ldots,\ y^{\mu}) \to J(P,X,y^1,y^2,\ \ldots,\ y^{\mu}):$$

$$H \to S,$$

We see that this mapping is single-valued and continuous. This is because med($\bar{w}$, $P_{o,1} + (X_{o,1} - \sum_{k=1}^{\mu} y_{o,1}^{k}), \hat{w})$, $\max(0, P_{o,j} + \nu(X_{o,j} - \sum_{k=1}^{\mu} y_{o,j}^{k} - \sum_{i=1}^{\ell} \bar{x}_{o,j}^{i} - \sum_{k=1}^{\mu} \bar{y}_{o,j}^{k}))$, *etc.*, are single-valued and continuous for each $(P, X, y^1, y^2, \ldots, y^\mu) \in H$.[133]

Now, forming the Cartesian product

$$\Phi(P,X,y^1,y^2,\ldots,y^\mu) = J(P,X,y^1,y^2,\ldots,y^\mu) \times \Gamma(P,X,y^1,y^2,\ldots,y^\mu) \times \bar{\eta}^1(P) \times \bar{\eta}^2(P) \times \ldots \times \bar{\eta}^\mu(P) \text{ for each } (P,X,y^1,y^2,\ldots,y^\mu) \in H,$$

construct the following Cartesian product of mappings:

$$(15.iii) \qquad (P,X,y^1,y^2,\ldots,y^\mu) \to \Phi(P,X,y^1,y^2,\ldots,y^\mu): H \to H.$$

The mapping H is closed, because H is the Cartesian product of $(2 + \mu)$ closed mappings.[134] Moreover, the image $\Phi(P,X,y^1,y^2,\ldots,y^\mu)$ is a convex subset of H.[135] Needless to say, H is a convex and compact set. Thus, by Kakutani's Fixed Point Theorem,[136] a fixed point $(P^o, X^o, y^{1^o}, y^{2^o}, \ldots, y^{\mu^o})$ exists. But, as each labourer already acts according to the dual-decision hypothesis, X^o is $\tilde{X}^o$ by definition. That is, there exists a fixed point $(P^o, \tilde{X}^o, y^{1^o}, y^{2^o}, \ldots, y^{\mu^o}) \in \Phi(P^o, \tilde{X}^o, y^{1^o}, y^{2^o}, \ldots, y^{\mu^o})$, where $P^o = J(P^o, \tilde{X}^o, y^{1^o}, y^{2^o}, \ldots, y^{\mu^o})$, $\tilde{X}^o \in \Gamma(P^o, \tilde{X}^o, y^{1^o}, y^{2^o}, \ldots, y^{\mu^o})$ and $y^{k^o} \in \bar{\eta}^k(P^o)$, $k=1,2,\ldots,\mu$.

The inequalities (15.iv) follow from (15.i):

$$(15.iv) \qquad P_{o,1}^{o} = \text{med}\{\bar{w}^o, P_{o,1}^{o} + (\tilde{X}_{o,1}^{o} - \sum_{k=1}^{\ell} y_{o,1}^{k^o}), \hat{w}\}$$

---

133. Cf. Nikaido, *op.cit.*, pp. 96-97 and Glustoff, *op.cit.*, footnote 3 on p. 332.
134. Cf. Nikaido, *op.cit.*, pp. 314-315.
135. Cf. Nikaido, *op.cit.*, p. 197.
136. Kakutani [12]

$$P^o_{o,j} \geqq \frac{1}{\theta}\{P^o_{o,j} + \nu(\tilde{X}^o_{o,j} - \sum_{k=1}^{\mu} y^{k^o}_{o,j} - \sum_{i=1}^{\ell} \bar{x}^i_{o,j}$$

$$- \sum_{k=1}^{\mu} \bar{y}^k_{o,j})\}, \quad j=2,3, \ldots, n$$

$$P^o_{o,n+1} \geqq \frac{1}{\theta}\{P^o_{o,n+1} + \nu(\tilde{X}^o_{o,n+1} + \sum_{k=1}^{\mu} y^{k^o}_{o,n+1})\}$$

$$\bar{z}^o \geqq \frac{1}{\theta}\{\bar{z}^o + \nu(\tilde{X}^o_{o,o} + \sum_{k=1}^{\mu} y^{k^o}_{o,o} - \bar{z}^o)\}.$$

Now we will investigate the sign of each element of the vector $P^o \in S$.

Since P^o satisfies the inequalities (β), obviously $P^o_{o,1} > 0$ and at least one element of $(P^o_{o,2}, P^o_{o,3}, \ldots, P^o_{o,n+1}, \bar{z}^o)$ is positive. Furthermore, it can be shown that all other prices $P^o_{o,j}$, as well as $\bar{z}^o$, are also positive.

a) Let us suppose that this positive element of $(P^o_{o,2}, P^o_{o,3}, \ldots, P^o_{o,n+1}, \bar{z}^o)$ is the price of the q-th real good, $P^o_{o,q}$ $(q \neq 1, q \neq n+1)$.

From Assumption II.1, we know that there is some rentier who has the q-th good. Thus we can infer that, for this rentier, there exists a demand or supply function not extended, *i.e.* (12.vi), defined by employing S^* of either (12.i) or (12.iii).[137] From this inference, the following three results can be derived.

a.i) All prices $P^o_{o,j}$ (j=2,3, ..., n) are positive.

That is, if any of the prices of real goods in a fixed point, say $P^o_{o,j}$, is zero, then it follows from the utility maximization behaviour and Assumption I.5 that $x^i_{o,j}$ increases without limit and reaches the upper bound of B^i which corresponds to the j-th good of the 0-th period. Thus, it follows from the

---

137. Cf. a) and c) on pp. 68-69.

definition of B^i that $(\tilde{X}^o_{o,j} - \sum_{k=1}^{\mu} y^{k^o}_{o,j} - \sum_{i=1}^{\ell} \bar{x}^i_{o,j} - \sum_{k=1}^{\mu} \bar{y}^k_{o,j})$ in the second inequality of (15.iv) becomes positive. Therefore, $P^o_{o,j}$ and hence all other prices $P^o_{o,j}$ $(j \neq 1, j \neq n+1)$, are positive.

a.ii) $P^o_{o,n+1}$ is also positive.

This positivity is verified as follows. Since $P^o_{o,j}$ $(j=1,2, \ldots, n)$ is positive, for every rentier who has some real good other than money stock and bonds (cf. Assumption II.1) there exists a demand or supply function not extended, which is defined by set S^* of (12.i) or (12.iii). Accordingly, we can infer that, if $P^o_{o,n+1}$ is zero, then a rentier, whose $\kappa^i_{t,b}$ $(t=0,1, \ldots, \tau-1)$ is equal to 1 (cf. Assumption IV.10), has an unlimited demand for bonds when the price $P^o_{o,n+1}$ is zero. Hence $x^{i^o}_{o,n+1}$ reaches the upper bound of B^i which corresponds to the bond of the 0-th period.[138] Thus, it follows from the definition of B^i that $(\tilde{X}^o_{o,n+1} + \sum_{k=1}^{\mu} y^o_{o,n+1})$ in the third inequality of (15.iv) becomes positive. Accordingly, $P^o_{o,n+1} > 0$, that is, the interest rate in the 0-th period is positive.

a.iii) $\bar{z}^o$ is positive.

This positivity is verified as follows. Since $P^o_{o,j}$ $(j=1,2, \ldots, n+1)$ is positive, every firm has a demand or supply function not extended, which is defined on S^{π}. Accordingly, in order to show the positivity of $\bar{z}^o$, we intend to compare the first inequality of the k-th firm's budget constraints (3)' with the first inequality of its money constraints (3.a)', where, for at least this firm, Assumption IV.7 is satisfied. That is,

---

138. It has often been asserted as self-evident that, when the price of bonds is zero, the demand for bonds becomes infinite. But, in the case of our model, the proof of its infinity is not easy, because our model has the set of money constraints and Assumption V.3. However, it follows from Assumption IV.10 that at least one rentier's demand for bonds becomes infinite. See Appendix IV.

$$(\gamma.\text{i}) \qquad P^o_{o,n+1}y^{k^o}_{o,n+1} + y^{k^o}_{o,o} \leqq \lambda^k\bar{z}^o + P^o_o\bar{y}^k_o.$$

$$(\gamma.\text{ii}) \qquad \begin{aligned} \max(P^o_{o,n+1}y^{k^o}_{o,n+1},0) \leqq\ & \lambda^k\bar{z}^o + \sum_{j\in I^k} P^o_{o,j}(\bar{\kappa}^k_{o,j}\bar{y}^k_{o,j} \\ & + \kappa^k_{o,j}y^{k^o}_{o,j}) + \sum_{j\in\tilde{I}^k}\max\{\kappa^k_{o,j}P^o_{o,j}(\bar{y}^k_{o,j} + y^{k^o}_{o,j}),0\} \\ & + \max(-\kappa^k_{o,n+1}P^o_{o,n+1}y^{k^o}_{o,n+1},0) - \sum_{j=1}^n\max\{-P^o_{o,j}\cdot \\ & (y^{k^o}_{o,j} + \bar{y}^k_{o,j}),0\}. \end{aligned}$$

Now, consider (γ.i) and (γ.ii) in two cases, 1) where $y^{k^o}_{o,n+1}$ is positive, and 2) where $y^{k^o}_{o,n+1}$ is non-positive, respectively.

1) If $y^{k^o}_{o,n+1}$ is positive, then the fourth term of the right-hand side of (γ.ii), *i.e.*, $\max(-\kappa^k_{o,n+1}P^o_{o,n+1}y^{k^o}_{o,n+1},0)$, is zero, and the fifth term, *i.e.* $-\sum_{j=1}^n\max\{-P^o_{o,j}(y^{k^o}_{o,j} + \bar{y}^k_{o,k}),0\}$, is non-positive. Moreover, $y^{k^o}_{o,j}$ in the third term is non-positive, as it is the net input. Accordingly, taking into account the positivity of $P^o_o\bar{y}^k_o$ in (γ.i)[139] and Assumption IV.7,[140] we see that the value of the right-hand side of (γ.i) is greater than the value of the right-hand side of (γ.ii). Thus, when $y^{k^o}_{o,o}$ is zero, it is impossible for (γ.i) to hold in equality while (γ.ii) holds in strict inequality. Therefore, only the following two cases are possible:

---

139. $P^o_o\bar{y}^k_o$ is positive because $\bar{y}^k_o \geq 0$ by virtue of Assumption II.3 and $P^o_o > 0$ as has already been verified, where P^o_o is the row vector $(P^o_{o,2}, P^o_{o,3}, \ldots, P^o_{o,n})$ in the fixed point. (Cf. p. 7 above for the notation of P_o.)

140. By virtue of Assumption IV.7, $\bar{\kappa}^k_{o,j}$ in the second term of the right-hand side of (γ.ii) is smaller than 1, $\kappa^k_{o,j}$ in the same term is zero, and $\kappa^k_{o,j}$ in the third term is smaller than 1.

i) the inequalities (γ.i) and (γ.ii) both hold in strict inequality, or

ii) only the inequality (γ.i) holds in strict inequality.

In both cases i) and ii), $y^{k^o}_{o,o}$ must be positive due to the positivity of the right-hand side of (γ.i). We can make this inference because the firm can obtain a greater present value (1.iii) by increasing $y^{k^o}_{o,o}$ above zero and then by appropriately increasing $y^{k^o}_{t,o}$ ($t=1,2, \ldots, \tau-1$), without violating the sets of constraints (3)', (3.a)', (3.b), (3.c), and (3.d).[141] The possibility of obtaining a greater present value in this manner is evident from the definition of $\beta^k (\beta^k = y^k_{\tau-1,n+1} + y^k_{\tau-1,o})$ and because $P_{o,n+1}$ and all $P^k_{t,n+1}$'s ($t=1, \ldots, \tau-1$) are positive.[142] Thus, $y^{k^o}_{o,o} > 0$.[143]

2) If $y^{k^o}_{o,n+1}$ is non-positive, then let us shift the term $P^o_{o,n+1} y^{k^o}_{o,n+1}$ to the right-hand side of (γ.i), and consider (γ.i)' and (γ.ii)':

$$(\gamma.\mathrm{i})' \quad y^{k^o}_{o,o} \leqq \lambda^{k^o} \bar{z} + P^o_o \bar{y}^k_o - P^o_{o,n+1} y^{k^o}_{o,n+1}.$$

$$(\gamma.\mathrm{ii})' \quad 0 \leqq \lambda^{k^o} \bar{z} + \sum_{j \in I^k} P^o_{o,j} (\bar{\kappa}^k_{o,j} \bar{y}^k_{o,k} + \kappa^k_{o,j} y^{k^o}_{o,j})$$

$$+ \sum_{j \in \tilde{I}^k} \max\{\kappa^k_{o,j} P^o_{o,j} (\bar{y}^k_{o,j} + y^{k^o}_{o,j}), 0\}$$

---

141. Even though we increase $y^{k^o}_{o,o}$ above zero, and then increase $y^{k^o}_{t,o}$ ($t=1,2, \ldots, \tau-1$), y^k can still belong to the set A^k, since all elements of y^k, except $y^k_{o,o}$ and $y^k_{t,o}$ ($t=1,2, \ldots, \tau-1$), are kept unchanged.

142. Since it was shown that $P^o_{o,n+1} > 0$, the positivity of $P^k_{t,n+1}$ ($t=1,2, \ldots, \tau-1$) is clear by Assumption VIII.2.

143. This proof of the positivity of the demand for money stocks is based on an important suggestion by Mr. R. Okumura, a graduate student in the Department of Economics of Tohoku University. Previously I had tried to accomplish my proof by setting up an assumption on a household's utility function (Haga [6] and [7]). Although Mr. Okumura also sets up such an assumption, he called attention to one of

$$+ \max(-\kappa^{k}_{o,n+1}P^{o}_{o,n+1}y^{k^o}_{o,n+1},0) - \sum_{j=1}^{n}\max\{-P^{o}_{o,j}\cdot (y^{k^o}_{o,j} + \bar{y}^{k}_{o,j}),0\}.$$

Since all other conditions remain unchanged, again the value of the right-hand side of (γ.i)' is likewise greater than the value of the right-hand side of (γ.ii)'. Accordingly, for the same reasons stated above, it is impossible for $y^{k^o}_{o,o}$ to be zero. Hence, $y^{k^o}_{o,o} > 0$.

Thus, in both cases 1) and 2), $y^{k^o}_{o,o}$ must be positive. Therefore, since $(\tilde{X}^{o}_{o,o} + \sum_{k=1}^{\mu} y^{k^o}_{o,o} - \bar{z}^{o})$ in the fourth inequality of (15.iv) is positive, necessarily $\bar{z}^{o} > 0$. Consequently, from discussions (a.i),(a.ii), and (a.iii), we can say that

$$P^{o}_{o,j} > 0, \quad j=1,2, \ldots, n+1, \text{ and } \bar{z}^{o} > 0.$$

b) Let us suppose that the positive element of $(P^{o}_{o,2}, P^{o}_{o,3}, \ldots, P^{o}_{o,n+1}, \bar{z}^{o})$ is the price of a bond, $P^{o}_{o,n+1}$.

From Assumption IV.9, we know that there is at least one rentier i for whom $0 < \kappa^{i}_{t,n+1} < 1$, $t=0,1, \ldots, \tau-1$. Thus we can infer that, for this rentier, there exists a demand or supply function not extended, *i.e.* (12.vi), defined by employing S^{*} of either (12.i) or (12.ii).[144] From this inference, the following three results can be derived.

b.i) All prices $P^{o}_{o,j}$ (j=2,3, ..., n) are positive. (It has already been shown that $P^{o}_{o,1} > 0$.)

---

the essential points of the problem, *i.e.*, that the demand for money stocks is positive. This led me to adopt an assumption on a firm's production instead of on a household's utility function. (Cf. Mr. Okumura's forthcoming article, "Transaction Cost and Monetary Equilibrium", in Japanese.)

144. Cf. a) and b) on pp. 68-69. See Appendix II for the existence of demand or supply function not extended.

b.ii) $P^o_{o,n+1} > 0$, as already supposed.

b.iii) $\bar{z}^o > 0$.

Since the proofs of (b.i) and (b.iii) are entirely the same as those of (a.i) and (a.iii) respectively, they will be omitted.

c) Let us suppose that the positive element of $(P^o_{o,2}, P^o_{o,3}, \ldots, P^o_{o,n+1}, \bar{z}^o)$ is $\bar{z}^o$.

From Assumption II.1, we know that there is at least one rentier i who has money stock as his initial holding in the 0-th period. Thus we can infer that, for this rentier, there exists a demand or supply function not extended, *i.e.* (12.vi), defined by employing S^* of either (12.ii) or (12.iv).[145] From this inference, the following three results can be derived:

c.i) All prices $P^o_{o,j}$ (j=2,3, ..., n) are positive. (It has already been shown that $P^o_{o,1} > 0$.)

c.ii) $P^o_{o,n+1} > 0$.

c.iii) $\bar{z}^o > 0$, as already supposed.

Since the proofs of (c.i) and (c.ii) are the same as those of (a.i) and (a.ii) respectively, they will be omitted. Thus in all cases of (a), (b), and (c), all $P^o_{o,j}$'s (j=1,2, ..., n+1) and $\bar{z}^o$ are positive.[146]

From the positivity of all $P^o_{o,j}$'s (j=1,2, ..., n+1) and $\bar{z}^o$, we can confirm that there exist all demand or supply functions not extended, which are defined for the vector $(P^o_{o,1}, P^o_{o,2}, P^o_{o,3}, \ldots, P^o_{o,n+1}, \bar{z}^o)$. Since these functions not extended are the

---

145. Cf. b) and d) on pp. 69-70.

146. Note that the problem of the case where $\bar{Z}_o = 0$ in function W of Assumption VII.a) is eliminated because $\bar{z}^o$ is positive. Cf. footnote 113 pp. 70-71.

mappings (10.ii),(11.ii)', and (12.vi), of firms, labourers, and rentiers, we need consider only these mappings which are not extended.

The following relations are derived from the first equality of (15.iv):

$$\text{(i)}\qquad \bar{w} \leqq P^o_{o,1} = P^o_{o,1} + (\tilde{X}^o_{o,1} - \sum_{k=1}^{\mu} y^{k^o}_{o,1}) \leqq \hat{w}.$$

$$\text{(ii)}\qquad \bar{w} < P^o_{o,1} = \hat{w} \leqq P^o_{o,1} + (\tilde{X}^o_{o,1} - \sum_{k=1}^{\mu} y^{k^o}_{o,1}).$$

$$\text{(iii)}\qquad P^o_{o,1} + (\tilde{X}^o_{o,1} - \sum_{k=1}^{\mu} y^{k^o}_{o,1}) \leqq P^o_{o,1} = \bar{w} < \hat{w}.$$

From (i) we see that $\tilde{X}^o_{o,o} - \sum_{k=1}^{\mu} y^{k^o}_{o,1} = 0$. From (ii), we see that $\tilde{X}^o_{o,o} - \sum_{k=1}^{\mu} y^{k^o}_{o,1} = 0$, because $\sum_{k=1}^{\mu} y^{k^o}_{o,1}$ is zero at $P^o_{o,1} = \hat{w}$ by virtue of Assumption III.5 and because $\tilde{X}^o_{o,1}$ is zero by virtue of Assumption X or (13.ix). Also, from (iii), we know that $\tilde{X}^o_{o,1} - \sum_{k=1}^{\mu} y^{k^o}_{o,1} = 0$ because $\tilde{X}^o_{o,1} - \sum_{k=1}^{\mu} y^{k^o}_{o,1} \geqq 0$ by virtue of the new definition of the total labour supply, (13.vii), based on the dual-decision hypothesis. Thus, in all cases,

$$\tilde{X}^o_{o,1} - \sum_{k=1}^{\mu} y^{k^o}_{o,1} = 0.$$

Now, taking into consideration (15.i) as well as the positivity of all $P^o_{o,j}$'s and $\bar{z}^o$, (15.iv) becomes (15.v). That is

$$\text{(15.v)}\qquad P^o_{o,1}(\tilde{X}^o_{o,1} - \sum_{k=1}^{\mu} y^{k^o}_{o,1}) = 0, \quad P^o_{o,1} > 0;$$

$$P^o_{o,j} = \frac{1}{\theta}\{P^o_{o,j} + \nu(\tilde{X}^o_{o,j} - \sum_{k=1}^{\mu} y^{k^o}_{o,j} - \sum_{i=1}^{\ell} \bar{x}^i_{o,j} - \sum_{k=1}^{\mu} \bar{y}^k_{o,j})\}, \quad j=2,3,\ \dots,\ n;$$

$$P^o_{o,n+1} = \frac{1}{\theta}\{P^o_{o,n+1} + \nu(\tilde{X}^o_{o,n+1} + \sum_{k=1}^{\mu} y^{k^o}_{o,n+1})\};$$

$$\bar{z}^o = \frac{1}{\theta}\{\bar{z}^o + \nu(\tilde{X}^o_{o,o} + \sum_{k=1}^{\mu} y^{k^o}_{o,o} - \bar{z}^o)\}.$$

Also, since the demand or supply function of each firm is the one not extended, $P^o_o y^{k^o}_o$ is non-negative due to the firm's maximization behaviour, and hence $\max(\sum_{k=1}^{\mu}\alpha^i_{o,k} P^o_o y^{k^o}_o, 0) = \sum_{k=1}^{\mu}\alpha^i_{o,k}\pi^o_{o,k}$.[147] Accordingly, (2.ii)" reverts to (2.ii)'.

If we add up all budget constraints in the 0-th period of (2.i)',(2.ii)', and (3)', the inequality (15.vi) follows from $\sum_{i=1}^{\ell}\lambda^i + \sum_{k=1}^{\mu}\lambda^k = 1$, $\sum_{i=h+1}^{\ell}\alpha^i_{o,k} = 1$, and $\pi^o_{o,k} = P^o_o y^{k^o}_o$:

$$\text{(15.vi)} \quad \sum_{i=1}^{h} P^o_o \tilde{x}^{i^o}_o + \sum_{i=h+1}^{\ell} P^o_o x^{i^o}_o + P^o_{o,n+1}\Big(\sum_{i=1}^{\ell}\tilde{x}^{i^o}_{o,n+1} + \sum_{k=1}^{\mu} y^{k^o}_{o,n+1}\Big)$$

$$+ \sum_{i=1}^{\ell}\tilde{x}^{i^o}_{o,o} + \sum_{i=h+1}^{\ell} x^{i^o}_{o,o} + \sum_{k=1}^{\mu} y^{k^o}_{o,o}$$

$$\leqq \bar{z}^o + \sum_{i=1}^{\ell} P^o_o \bar{x}^i_o + \sum_{k=1}^{\mu} P^o_o \bar{y}^k_o + \sum_{k=1}^{\mu} P^o_o y^{k^o}_o .$$

The following equalities are derived from (15.v):

$$\text{(15.vii)} \quad 0 = P^o_{o,1}\Big(\tilde{X}^o_{o,1} - \sum_{k=1}^{\mu} y^{k^o}_{o,1}\Big);$$

$$P^{o^2}_{o,j}\Big(\frac{\theta-1}{\nu}\Big) = P^o_{o,j}\Big(\tilde{X}^o_{o,j} - \sum_{k=1}^{\mu} y^{k^o}_{o,j} - \sum_{i=1}^{\ell}\bar{x}^i_{o,j}$$

$$- \sum_{k=1}^{\mu}\bar{y}^k_{o,j}\Big), \quad j=2,3,\ \ldots,\ n;$$

$$P^{o^2}_{o,n+1}\Big(\frac{\theta-1}{\nu}\Big) = P^o_{o,n+1}\Big(\tilde{X}^o_{o,n+1} + \sum_{k=1}^{\mu} y^{k^o}_{o,n+1}\Big);$$

$$\bar{z}^o\Big(\frac{\theta-1}{\nu}\Big) = \Big(\tilde{X}^o_{o,o} + \sum_{k=1}^{\mu} y^{k^o}_{o,o} - \bar{z}^o\Big).$$

From (15.vii) we will show that $\theta = 1$.

i) If $\theta > 1$, then the values of each right-hand side of (15.vii), excluding the first equality, are positive. This contradicts the inequality of (15.vi)

---

147. $\pi^o_{o,k}$ is $\pi_{o,k}$ corresponding to the fixed point.

as can be seen if all the right-hand sides of (15.vii), including the first equality are added. Hence $\theta \leqq 1$.

ii) If $\theta < 1$, then the values of each right-hand side of (15.vii), excluding the first equality, are negative. Consequently, (15.vi) holds in strict inequality. Moreover, this strict inequality implies that the budget constraint in the 0-th period of at least one economic unit (labourer, rentier or firm) holds in strict inequality.

ii.α) Let us suppose that this economic unit is some rentier (or labourer) i. For this rentier (or labourer) $x^{i^o} \in L^i$ and hence $x^{i^o} \in V^o$. By appropriately increasing each $x^{i^o}_{o,o}, x^{i^o}_{1,o}, x^{i^o}_{2,o}, \ldots, x^{i^o}_{\tau-1,o}$ and $x^{i^o}_{\tau,j}$ [148] which are elements of x^{i^o}, we can find a new feasible solution x^{i^Δ} such that:

a) x^{i^Δ} satisfies (2.ii)" or (2.ii)', (2.ii.a)' and (2.ii.b) in the case of rentier, and (2.i)', (2.i.a)', and (2.i.b) in the case of labourer,

b) $x^{i^\Delta} \in V$, $x^{i^\Delta} \in M^i$ and hence $x^{i^\Delta} \in B^i$, and $U(x^{i^o}_o, x^{i^o}_1, \ldots, x^{i^o}_\tau) < U(x^{i^\Delta}_o, x^{i^\Delta}_1, \ldots, x^{i^\Delta}_\tau)$, from Assumption I.5.

This contradicts the definition of (12.v) (or (11.i)').

ii.β) Let us suppose that it is the k-th firm's budget constraint which holds with strict inequality in the 0-th period. For this firm, $y^{k^o} \in T^k$ and $y^{k^o} \in E^o$. By appropriately increasing each $y^{k^o}_{o,o}, y^{k^o}_{1,o}, \ldots,$ and $y^{k^o}_{\tau-1,o}$ which are elements of y^{k^o}, we can find a new feasible solution y^{k^Δ} such that:

---

148. The subscript j of $x^i_{\tau,j}$ is the j-th real good (j=2,3, ..., n) in the τ-th period.

a) $y^{k^{\Delta}}$ satisfies (3)',(3.a)',(3.b),(3.c), and (3.d), likewise

b) $y^{k^{\Delta}} \in E$, $y^{k^{\Delta}} \in N^k$ and hence $y^{k^{\Delta}} \in A^k$.

Now, from the definitions of the present value (1.iii) and of β^k, $y^{k^{\Delta}}$ generates a greater value than $y^{k^{o}}$. This contradicts the definition of (10.i). Hence $\theta \geqq 1$.

We have shown in i) that $\theta > 1$ is impossible. In ii) we have shown that $\theta < 1$ is impossible. Thus $\theta = 1$.

The following equalities (15.viii) are derived from (15.vii), taking into account the positivity of $P^o_{o,j}$ (j=1,2, ..., n+1) and $\bar{z}^o$, and the fact that $\theta = 1$.

(15.viii)
$$\tilde{X}^o_{o,1} - \sum_{k=1}^{\mu} y^{k^o}_{o,1} = 0;$$

$$\tilde{X}^o_{o,j} - \sum_{k=1}^{\mu} y^{k^o}_{o,j} - \sum_{i=1}^{\ell} \bar{x}^i_{o,j} - \sum_{k=1}^{\mu} \bar{y}^k_{o,j} = 0, \qquad j=2,3, \ldots, n;$$

$$\tilde{X}^o_{o,n+1} + \sum_{k=1}^{\mu} y^{k^o}_{o,n+1} = 0;$$

$$\tilde{X}^o_{o,o} + \sum_{k=1}^{\mu} y^{k^o}_{o,o} - \bar{z}^o = 0.$$

As will be seen, the first equality of (15.viii) represents the labour market equilibrium. The set of second equalities (j=2,3, ..., n) represents the product market equilibria. The fourth equality represents the normalized equilibrium of the money stock, but not the equilibrium of the money stock itself. The equilibrium of the money stock market can be found by multiplying each term of the left-hand side of the fourth equality of (15.viii) by some appropriate number which will convert the normalized $\bar{z}^o$ to the actual money stock $\bar{Z}_o$. Similarly, the third equality of (15.viii) is the normalized equilibrium of the bond market, but not the equilibrium of the bond market itself. Through an analogous procedure, we can easily find the equilibrium of the bond market, as will be shown below.

However, above all, it must be kept in mind that our model until now has been based on demand or supply functions being modified by restricting the original choice sets of economic units. Accordingly, we must prove that market equilibria hold even in the original model where the demand or supply functions are not so modified.

4. The Existence Proof (2)

— The Original Model (Non-Modified Functions) based on the Dual-Decision Hypothesis —

i) Suppose that, for the k-th firm, there is a vector y^{k^α}, not belonging to A^k, which has the following properties :

a) $y^{k^\alpha} \in N^k$,

b) y^{k^α} satisfies (3)',(3.a)',(3.b),(3.c), and (3.d), and

c)
$$P^o_o y^{k^\alpha}_o + P^o_{o,n+1} P^k_1 y^{k^\alpha}_1 + P^o_{o,n+1} P^k_{1,n+1} P^k_2 y^{k^\alpha}_2 + \dots + P^o_{o,n+1} P^k_{1,n+1} \times \dots \times P^k_{\tau-1,n+1} (P^k_\tau y^{k^\alpha}_\tau + y^{k^\alpha}_{\tau-1,n+1} + y^{k^\alpha}_{\tau-1,o}) > P^o_o y^{k^o}_o + P^o_{o,n+1} P^k_1 y^{k^o}_1 + P^o_{o,n+1} P^k_{1,n+1} P^k_2 y^{k^o}_2 + \dots + P^o_{o,n+1} P^k_{1,n+1} \times \dots \times P^k_{\tau-1,n+1} (P^k_\tau y^{k^o}_\tau + y^{k^o}_{\tau-1,n+1} + y^{k^o}_{\tau-1,o}) = \Pi^o_{o,k},$$

where $\Pi^o_{o,k}$ is $\Pi_{o,k}$ corresponding to the fixed point.

As can be easily seen, any vector y^{k^β} on the segment $[y^{k^o}, y^{k^\alpha}]$ satisfies (3)', (3.a)',(3.b),(3.c), and (3.d).[149] Since $y^{k^o} \in A^k = N^k \cap E$, $y^{k^\alpha} \in N^k$, and since N^k is convex, $y^{k^\beta} \in N^k$. Also, since $y^{k^o} \in T^k$, $y^{k^o} \in E^o$. Hence, $y^{k^o} \in N^k \cap E^o$. If y^{k^β} is taken sufficiently close to y^{k^o}, $y^{k^\beta} \in N^k \cap E = A^k$. Then, the following ine-

149. See Appendix III for proof that y^{k^β} satisfies the non-linear inequality (3.a)'.

quality holds :

$$\text{(16.ii)} \quad P^o_o y^{k^\beta}_o + P^o_{o,n+1} P^k_1 y^{k^\beta}_1 + P^o_{o,n+1} P^k_{1,n+1} P^k_2 y^{k^\beta}_2 + \ldots\ldots + P^o_{o,n+1} P^k_{1,n+1} \times \ldots\ldots\ldots \times P^k_{\tau-1,n+1} (P^k_\tau y^{k^\beta}_\tau + y^{k^\beta}_{\tau-1,n+1} + y^{k^\beta}_{\tau-1,o}) > \Pi^o_{o,k}.$$

This inequality contradicts the definition of y^{k^o} ($y^{k^o} \in \Omega^k$ (P^o) for $P^o \in S^\pi$).[150]

Thus, y^{k^o} is the k-th firm's maximal solution, subject only to (3)',(3.a)',(3.b), (3.c),(3.d), and $y^{k^\alpha} \in N^k$. Therefore, y^{k^o} is the k-th firm's maximal solution even in the original, unrestricted, choice set.

ii) Suppose that, for the i-th labourer, there is a vector $\tilde{x}^{i^\alpha}$, not belonging to B^i, which has the following properties:[151]

a) $\tilde{x}^{i^\alpha} \in M^i$,

b) $\tilde{x}^{i^\alpha}$ satisfies (2.i)",(2.i.a)', and (2.i.b), and

c) $U^i(\tilde{x}^{i^\alpha}_o, \tilde{x}^{i^\alpha}_1, \ldots, \tilde{x}^{i^\alpha}_\tau) > U^i(\tilde{x}^{i^o}_o, \tilde{x}^{i^o}_1, \ldots, \tilde{x}^{i^o}_\tau)$.

As can be easily seen any vector $\tilde{x}^{i^\beta}$ on the segment $[\tilde{x}^{i^o}, \tilde{x}^{i^\alpha}]$ satisfies (2.i)" (2.i)",(2.i.a)', and (2.i.b).[152] Since $\tilde{x}^{i^o} \in B^i = M^i \cap V$, $\tilde{x}^{i^\alpha} \in M^i$ and since M^i is convex, $\tilde{x}^{i^\beta} \in M^i$. Also, since $\tilde{x}^{i^o} \in L^i$, $\tilde{x}^{i^o} \in V^o$. Hence $\tilde{x}^{i^o} \in M^i \cap V^o$. If $\tilde{x}^{i^\beta}$ is

---

150. Cf. (10.i) on p. 58.

151. $\tilde{x}^{i^\alpha}$ is the i-th labourer's solution based on the dual-decision hypothesis. (Cf. p. 76 for the notation ~.) On the other hand, x^{i^α} is the i-th rentier's solution, not based on the dual-decision hypothesis.

152. See Appendix III for proof that $\tilde{x}^{i^\beta}$ satisfies the non-linear inequality (2.i.a)'.

taken sufficiently close to $\tilde{x}^{i^o}$, $\tilde{x}^{i^\beta} \in M^i \cap V = B^i$. Then, from Assumptions I.3 and I.4, the following inequality is derived :

$$(16.\text{iii}) \qquad U^i(\tilde{x}_o^{i^\beta}, \tilde{x}_1^{i^\beta}, \ldots, \tilde{x}_\tau^{i^\beta}) > U^i(\tilde{x}_o^{i^o}, \tilde{x}_1^{i^o}, \ldots, \tilde{x}_\tau^{i^o}).$$

This inequality contradicts the definition of $\tilde{x}^{i^o}$ ($\tilde{x}^{i^o} \in \tilde{f}^i(P^o)$ for $P^o \in S^o$).[153] Accordingly, independently of whether or not $\tilde{x}^{i^o}$ belongs to B^i, $\tilde{x}^{i^o}$ is the i-th labourer's maximal solution, subject to only (2.i)",(2.i.a)',(2.i.b), and $\tilde{x}^{i^o} \in M^i$. Therefore, $\tilde{x}^{i^o}$ is the i-th labourer's maximal solution, even in the original, unrestricted, set.

iii) Suppose that, for the i-th rentier, there is a vector x^{i^α}, not belonging to B^i, which has the following properties.

a) $x^{i^\alpha} \in M^i$,

b) x^{i^α} satisfies (2.ii)" or (2.ii)',(2.ii.a)', and (2.ii.b), and

c) $U^i(x_o^{i^\alpha}, x_1^{i^\alpha}, \ldots, x_\tau^{i^\alpha}) > U^i(x_o^{i^o}, x_1^{i^o}, \ldots, x_\tau^{i^o})$.

By the same method as employed in ii), we see that supposition iii) contradicts the definition of x^{i^o} ($x^{i^o} \in \psi^i(P, y^1, y^2, \ldots, y^\mu)$ for $(P^o, y^{1^o}, y^{2^o}, \ldots, y^{\mu^o}) \in S^* \times \Xi$).[154] Thus, in the case of any firm, labourer, or rentier, we can confirm that y^{k^o}, $\tilde{x}^{i^o}$ and x^{i^o} are, respectively, the maximal solutions for each economic unit's original, unrestricted, choice set.

Since $\bar{z}^o$ is positive as shown above, and since $\bar{Z}_o$ is positive from Assumption II.4, $\gamma\bar{z}^o = \bar{Z}_o$ for a positive number γ. Accordingly, equilibrium prices of real

---

153. Cf. (11.i)' on p. 76.
154. Cf. (12.v) on p. 71.

goods including labour, $P^*_{o,j}$, are:

$$P^*_{o,j} = \gamma P^o_{o,j}, \quad j=1,2, \ldots, n;$$

where $P^*_{o,1} \geqq \gamma \bar{w}^o$.[155]

The equilibrium price of bonds, $P^*_{o,n+1}$, is :

$$P^*_{o,n+1} = P^o_{o,n+1}.$$

The equilibrium quantities of demand for (or supply of) bonds by labourers ($\tilde{x}^{i^*}_{t,n+1}$) by rentiers ($x^{i^*}_{t,n+1}$), and by firms ($y^{k^*}_{t,n+1}$) are as follows :

$$\tilde{x}^{i^*}_{t,n+1} = \gamma \tilde{x}^{i^o}_{t,n+1}, \quad i=1,2, \ldots, h; \; t=0,1, \ldots, \tau-1;$$

$$x^{i^*}_{t,n+1} = \gamma x^{i^o}_{t,n+1}, \quad i=h+1,h+2, \ldots, \ell; \; t=0,1, \ldots, \tau-1;$$

$$y^{k^*}_{t,n+1} = \gamma y^{k^o}_{t,n+1}, \quad k=1,2, \ldots, \mu; \; t=0,1, \ldots, \tau-1.$$

The equilibrium quantities of labourer's, rentier's, and firm's demand for money stocks, $\tilde{x}^{i^*}_{t,o}$, $x^{i^*}_{t,o}$ and $y^{k^*}_{t,o}$ are :

$$\tilde{x}^{i^*}_{t,o} = \gamma \tilde{x}^{i^o}_{t,o}, \quad i=1,2, \ldots, h; \; t=0,1, \ldots, \tau-1;$$

$$x^{i^*}_{t,o} = \gamma x^{i^o}_{t,o}, \quad i=h+1,h+2, \ldots, \ell; \; t=0,1, \ldots, \tau-1;$$

$$y^{k^*}_{t,o} = \gamma y^{k^o}_{t,o}, \quad k=1,2, \ldots, \mu; \; t=0,1, \ldots, \tau-1.$$

The expected prices of real goods in the equilibrium, $P^{i^*}_{t,j}$ and $P^{k^*}_{t,j}$, except for the expected price of bonds, after the 0-th period are obtained from Assumption VIII.4 as follows :

$$P^{i^*}_{t,j} = \gamma P^{i^o}_{t,j}, \quad i=1,2, \ldots, \ell;$$

---

155. $\bar{w}^o$ is $\bar{w}$ corresponding to the fixed point.

$$P^{k^*}_{t,j} = \gamma P^{k^o}_{t,j}, \quad k=1,2, \ldots, \mu;\ t=1,2, \ldots, \tau.$$

The expected prices of bonds in the equilibrium, $P^{i^*}_{t,n+1}$ and $P^{k^*}_{t,n+1}$ are :[156]

$$P^{i^*}_{t,n+1} = P^{i^o}_{t,n+1},$$

$$P^{k^*}_{t,n+1} = P^{k^o}_{t,n+1}, \quad t=1,2, \ldots, \tau-1.$$

Needless to say, these equilibrium prices, equilibrium quantities, and expected prices satisfy the budget constraints, money constraints, and other constraints. Also, as will be easily seen, at these equilibrium prices, equilibrium quantities, and expected prices, all firms and households retain their subjective equilibria.

As a result of the above, our general market equilibria are as follows :

$$\tilde{X}^*_{o,1} - \sum_{k=1}^{\mu} y^{k^*}_{o,1} = 0;$$

$$\tilde{X}^*_{o,j} - \sum_{k=1}^{\mu} y^{k^*}_{o,j} - \sum_{i=1}^{\ell} \bar{x}^{i}_{o,j} - \sum_{k=1}^{\mu} \bar{y}^{k}_{o,j} = 0, \quad j=2,3, \ldots, n;$$

$$\tilde{X}^*_{o,n+1} + \sum_{k=1}^{\mu} y^{k^*}_{o,n+1} = 0;$$

$$\tilde{X}^*_{o,o} + \sum_{k=1}^{\mu} y^{k^*}_{o,o} - \bar{Z}_o = 0,$$

where $\tilde{X}^*_{o,1} = \tilde{X}^o_{o,1}$, $\sum_{k=1}^{\mu} y^{k^*}_{o,1} = \sum_{k=1}^{\mu} y^{k^o}_{o,1}$, $\tilde{X}^*_{o,j} = \tilde{X}^o_{o,j} = \sum_{i=1}^{h} x^{i^o}_{o,j} + \sum_{i=h+1}^{\ell} x^{i^o}_{o,j} (j \neq n+1)$, $\tilde{X}^*_{o,n+1} = \sum_{i=1}^{h} \tilde{x}^{i^*}_{o,n+1} + \sum_{i=h+1}^{\ell} x^{i^*}_{o,n+1}$, and $\tilde{X}^*_{o,o} = \sum_{i=1}^{h} \tilde{x}^{i^*}_{o,o} + \sum_{i=h+1}^{\ell} x^{i^*}_{o,o}$.

Thus, as this chapter shows, the market equilibria hold, even in the original model where demand or supply functions are not modified.

---

156. Expected prices, $P^{i^*}_{t,n+1}$ and $P^{k^*}_{t,n+1}$, corresponding to the fixed point, are determined by Assumption VIII.4.

CHAPTER V

CONCLUSIONS

In the preceding chapter, we constructed modified demand or supply functions based on the dual-decision hypothesis by restricting the original choice sets. Then, we proved the existence of general equilibrium with unmodified functions which were still based on the dual-decision hypothesis. Also, we have proved not only that the prices of all goods are positive, but also that the interest rate is positive.

We have tried to combine the Walrasian system with the Keynesian system which has been reinterpreted by our version of the dual-decision hypothesis.[157] The dual-decision hypothesis employed in the present monograph is based on Clower's and Glustoff's reinterpretation of Keynes; their hypothesis, with my revision, may offer new possibilities for disequilibrium analysis. One way to develop this disequilibrium analysis is to apply the dual-decsion hypothesis to other markets as well as to the labour market. In such an application, it is important that the dual-decision hypothesis, on which economic units act, has as its basis some optimization principle. For example, Glustoff's hypothesis is based on his Lemma 1. (Cf. Glustoff, *op. cit.*, pp. 329-330.) Even though the dual-decision hypothesis is applied to other markets as well, if it does not intrinsically contain some optimization principle, the hypothesis will have relatively little economic meaning.

Our model differs from Walras' system primarily in its use of the dual-decision hypothesis. It also includes each unit's money constraints and other constraints, as well as a bond market, none of which is included in Walras' system. Nevertheless, our model is still a Walrasian general equilibrium model in that the interrelationship of all markets in the whole economic system is explicitly considered. Thus, our system combines the essence of Walras' system with a reinterpretation of Keynes'. However, our use of Walrasian equilibrium analysis still leaves some problems for future consideration.

---

157. Cf. pp. 32-33 above.

First, we attempted to verify the finiteness of bond demand and supply, only from within the economic system itself, without considering factors such as "transaction cost". This verification was extremely difficult and as a result, we were obliged to adopt Assumption V.3. However, it would have been preferable to derive the finiteness of bond demand and supply without resorting to this type of external assumption. This problem remains to be solved.

Second, our model is a type of dynamic model which includes the intertemporal planning time horizon. However, we treat only the equilibrium of the spot market, not those of the futures markets. While such treatment generally facilitated discussion, it required that we adopt Assumption IX.3, which would not have been necessary had we included the equilibria of the futures markets. Therefore, the problem of investigating the equilibria of both the spot market and the futures markets also remains to be solved.

Finally, $\kappa^i_{t,j}, \kappa^k_{t,n+1}, \kappa^i_{t,b}$, etc., in the money constraints are constant numbers, given beforehand. But, in fact, they must be decided in mutual relationship with other economic quantities and factors. This problem also remains.

APPENDIX I*

1. We will prove that $T^k_{o,n+1}(k=1,2, \ldots, \mu)$ is bounded and that $T^k_{t,n+1}$ is also bounded for each k and each $t(t=1,2, \ldots, \tau-1)$.

As we employ a successive method, first we will show that $y^k_{o,n+1}$ cannot be $-\infty$. Let us examine the second inequality of money constraints (3.a)'. As in the case with labourers and rentiers, we have only to consider the case where $\kappa^k_{1,n+1} P^k_{1,n+1}$ is not zero. From (3.b), if $y^k_{o,n+1}$ is $-\infty$, then $y^k_{1,n+1}$ must be $-\infty$ as well. Then, from the second inequality of (3.a)' and from (3.b), the following inequality is derived :

$$(3.a)'(1) \qquad \begin{aligned} & y^k_{o,o} + \sum_{j=1}^{n} \max(\kappa^k_{1,j} P^k_{1,j} y^k_{1,j}, 0) - \sum_{j=1}^{n} \max(-P^k_{1,j} y^k_{1,j}, 0) \\ & \qquad + \kappa^k_{1,n+1} P^k_{1,n+1} \Delta \geqq - y^k_{o,n+1}(1-\kappa^k_{1,n+1} P^k_{1,n+1}). \end{aligned}$$

Needless to say,

$$y^k_1 \in Q^k_1, \text{ where } y^k_1 = (y^k_{1,1}, y^k_{1,2}, \ldots, y^k_{1,n}).$$

It is clear from the positivity of $(1-\kappa^k_{1,n+1} P^k_{1,n+1})$ that if $y^k_{o,n+1}$ becomes $-\infty$, then necessarily the left-hand side of (3.a)'(1) must become $+\infty$. However, since $y^k_{o,o}(\geqq 0)$ has an upper bound and $\kappa^k_{1,n+1} P^k_{1,n+1}$ is a constant, $\sum_{j=1}^{n} \max(\kappa^k_{1,j} P^k_{1,j} y^k_{1,j}, 0)$ must become $+\infty$.

For simplicity, let us omit subscript k. Now, if $y_{o,n+1} \to -\infty$, then we have a sequence of vectors $\{(y^\nu_{o,n+1}, y^\nu_{o,o}, y^\nu_{1,1}, y^\nu_{1,2}, \ldots, y^\nu_{1,n})\}$ such that $\lim_{\nu\to\infty} y^\nu_{o,n+1} = -\infty$ and, for some element of the ν-th production vector $y^\nu_1 = (y^\nu_{1,1}, y^\nu_{1,2}, \ldots, y^\nu_{1,n}) \in Q_1$, say $y^\nu_{1,j}$, $\lim_{\nu\to\infty} y^\nu_{1,j} = +\infty$, where ν represents the ν-th term of the sequence and $y^\nu_{1,1}$

---

* For some of our results in Appendix I we are greatly indebted to discussions with a graduate student, Mr. H. Sato.

represents labour input independent of the value of ν.[158] Thus, the norm of production vector $||y_1^\nu||$ is larger than 1 for $\nu \geqq \nu^o$, where ν^o is a sufficiently large number. By supposition, the following inequality also holds for $\nu \geqq \nu^o$,

$$\text{(3.a)'(1)'} \qquad \begin{aligned} & y_{o,o}^\nu + \sum_{j=1}^{n} \max(\kappa_{1,j}P_{1,j}y_{1,j}^\nu, 0) - \sum_{j=1}^{n} \max(-P_{1,j}y_{1,j}^\nu, 0) \\ & + \kappa_{1,n+1}P_{1,n+1}\,\Delta \geqq -y_{o,n+1}^\nu(1-\kappa_{1,n+1}P_{1,n+1}), \\ & \text{where } y_1^\nu \in Q_1. \end{aligned}$$

From the convexity of Q_1 containing the zero vector (Assumption III.1),

$(1 - \frac{1}{||y_1^\nu||})(0,0, \ldots, 0) + \frac{1}{||y_1^\nu||}(y_{1,1}^\nu, y_{1,2}^\nu, \ldots, y_{1,n}^\nu) = (\frac{y_{1,1}^\nu}{||y_1^\nu||}, \frac{y_{1,2}^\nu}{||y_1^\nu||}, \ldots, \frac{y_{1,n}^\nu}{||y_1^\nu||}) \in Q_1$ for any $\nu \geqq \nu^o$. Since the norm of all production vectors $(\frac{y_{1,1}^\nu}{||y_1^\nu||}, \frac{y_{1,2}^\nu}{||y_1^\nu||}, \ldots, \frac{y_{1,n}^\nu}{||y_1^\nu||})$ is equal to 1, they all belong to a compact set. Accordingly, there exists a convergent subsequence $\{\frac{y_1^{\nu'}}{||y_1^{\nu'}||}\} = \{(\frac{y_{1,1}^{\nu'}}{||y_1^{\nu'}||}, \frac{y_{1,2}^{\nu'}}{||y_1^{\nu'}||}, \ldots, \frac{y_{1,n}^{\nu'}}{||y_1^{\nu'}||})\}$.

Let this convergent subsequence be denoted by $\{\tilde{y}_1^{\nu'}\} = \{(\tilde{y}_{1,1}^{\nu'}, \tilde{y}_{1,2}^{\nu'}, \ldots, \tilde{y}_{1,n}^{\nu'})\}$ and let the limit point be denoted by $\tilde{y}_1^o = (\tilde{y}_{1,1}^o, \tilde{y}_{1,2}^o, \ldots, \tilde{y}_{1,n}^o)$. Since Q_1 is closed (cf. Assumption III.1), $\tilde{y}_1^o \in Q_1$. In the limit point, $\tilde{y}_{1,1}^o$ is zero because labour input has an upper and a lower bound due to (3.c). Obviously, $\lim_{\nu' \to \infty} \frac{y_{o,o}^{\nu'}}{||y_1^{\nu'}||}$ is zero, and, by virtue of Assumption III.4, $\tilde{y}_1^o$ has no positive element.

---

158. The same subscript $j(j \neq 1)$ may represent net output or net input, depending the value of ν.

Therefore, since $||\tilde{y}_1^o||$ has at least one element which has a definite and negative value,

$$\frac{y^{\nu'}_{o,o}}{||y_1^{\nu'}||} + \sum_{j=1}^{n}\max(\kappa_{1,j}P_{1,j}\frac{y^{\nu'}_{1,j}}{||y_1^{\nu'}||}, 0) - \sum_{j=1}^{n}\max(-P_{1,j}\frac{y^{\nu'}_{1,j}}{||y_1^{\nu'}||}, 0)$$

$$(3.a)'(1)'' \qquad + \frac{\kappa_{1,n+1}P_{1,n+1}\Delta}{||y_1^{\nu'}||} \geqq - \frac{y^{\nu'}_{o,n+1}}{||y_1^{\nu'}||}(1-\kappa_{1,n+1}P_{1,n+1}), \text{ where}$$

$$(\frac{y^{\nu'}_{1,1}}{||y_1^{\nu'}||}, \frac{y^{\nu'}_{1,2}}{||y_1^{\nu'}||}, \dots, \frac{y^{\nu'}_{1,n}}{||y_1^{\nu'}||}) \in Q_1.$$

In (3.a)'(1)", we see that there is a sufficiently large number $\bar{\nu}'$ from definition of the limit point, such that the value of the left-hand side becomes negative for $\nu' \geqq \bar{\nu}'$. This is because $P_{1,j}$ has a maximum and a minimum value which are both positive for $j(j=1,2, \dots, n)$. On the other hand, the value of the right-hand side is always non-negative. These results violate (3.a)'(1)".

Accordingly, $y_{o,n+1}$ cannot be $-\infty$. That is, $y_{o,n+1}$ has a lower bound. This property of $y_{o,n+1}$ is independent of the expected prices $(P_{1,1}, P_{1,2}, \dots, P_{1,n}, P_{1,n+1})$, as long as $P_{1,j}(j=1,2, \dots, n)$ has a maximum and a minimum value which are both positive, and as long as $0 \leqq P_{1,n+1} \leqq 1$.[159] Furthermore, it is clear that $y_{o,n+1}$ also has an upper bound by virtue of the inequality (6).[160] This property is likewise independent of the expected prices.[161] Thus, $y_{o,n+1}$ is bounded. The boundedness of $T^k_{t,n+1}(t=1,2, \dots, \tau-1)$ is derived from (3.b), making use of the boundedness of $T^k_{o,n+1}$.

---

159. That the lower bound of $y_{o,n+1}$ can be chosen independently of these expected prices, can be easily verified.

160. Cf. footnote 73 on p. 46.

161. Again, this can be easily verified.

2. Next, we will prove that $T_t^k(k=1,2, \ldots, \mu; t=1,2, \ldots, \tau)$ is bounded.

This has already been proved implicitly in 1, but we will show it explicitly here. In order to show it, we need only to demonstrate that a firm can infinitely increase neither net output nor net input. If either net output or net input increases infinitely, then $\lim_{\nu'\to\infty} ||y_1^{\nu'}|| = +\infty$.

Now, from the boundedness of $T_{o,n+1}^k$, $\lim_{\nu'\to\infty} \frac{y_{o,n+1}^{\nu'}}{||y_1^{\nu'}||}$ is zero. All other conditions (including $0 \leqq y_{o,o} < \infty$) are the same as in 1. Thus, if $\nu' \to \infty$, the values of both sides of (3.a)'(1)" converge. The value of the left-hand side converges to a definite and negative value, and the value of the right-hand side converges to zero. These results violate (3.a)'(1)". That is, no firm can increase either net output or net input infinitely, while still satisfying the money constraints in which expected product prices are positive, and while still choosing production vectors which belong to Q_1. Therefore, as long as each firm must be subject to the constraints (3.c), as long as labour input has a lower bound, no firm can infinitely increase either net output or net input in the 1st period. However, by employing the third inequality of (3.a)' and the same properties of money stock demand, *etc.* (*e.g.* $0 \leqq y_{1,o} < \infty$), we can show that no firm can infinitely increase either net output or net input in the 2nd period, as well. Similarly, by applying the same method successively to each period $t(t=3,4, \ldots, \tau)$, the same conclusion is derived, making use of the fact that $y_{t,o}(t=2,3, \ldots, \tau-1)$ has an upper bound and a lower bound.[162] Moreover, these conclusions are independent of the expected prices, as long as $P_{t,j}(t=1,2, \ldots, \tau; j=1,2, \ldots, n)$ has a maximum and a minimum value which

---

162. As for firms, the boundedness of $T_{t,o}^k(t=1,2, \ldots, \tau-1)$ can be directly derived from (3)', because the boundedness of $T_{t,n+1}^k(t=0,1, \ldots, \tau-1)$ and $T_{o,o}^k$ were already shown. Accordingly, the boundedness of $T_t^k(t=1,2, \ldots, \tau)$ can be generally derived from the money constraint in the t-th period $(t=1,2, \ldots, \tau)$, without using the successive method.

are both positive, and as long as $0 \leqq P_{t,n+1} \leqq 1$ $(t=1,2, \ldots, \tau-1)$, as is the case with 1. Accordingly, $T_t^k (t=1,2, \ldots, \tau)$ is bounded. (The boundedness of T_o^k was already shown in Lemma I.)

APPENDIX II

A mapping is continuous if, and only if, it is both upper semi-continuous and lower semi-continuous, as stated above. The proof and examples that a mapping is upper semi-continuous are found in many sources. Therefore, in this appendix, we will show the essence of the proof of lower semi-continuity, based on the example in the present article.

(a) The Labourers' Case

We will show the lower semi-continuity of mapping (11.iii) defined for each $P \in S^o$. If we let the elements $x^i_{t,o}$ $(t=0,1, \ldots, \tau-1)$ of vector x^i be respectively appropriate positive numbers, and if, at the same time, we let the other elements of x^i be zero, then we can find an $x^i \in B^i$ such that :

(i) x^i satisfies the set of budget constraints (2.i)' in strict inequality, which is possible because the right-hand side of the first inequality of (2.i)' is positive by virtue of Assumption II.1,

(ii) x^i satisfies the set of money constraints (2.i.a)' in strict inequality due to Assumption IV.6, and

(iii) x^i satisfies the inequalities (2.i.b) not necessarily in strict inequality.

Theorem A 1. of Haga and Otsuki (*op. cit.* pp. 122-123) proves that the existence of at least one such feasible solution ensures the lower semi-continuity. (See also footnote 13 of the same article p. 122.) Then, utilize the convexity of the set of feasible solutions of the non-linear inequalities (2.i.a)' to finish the proof of the lower semi-continuity of mapping (11.iii). (Cf. Appendix III.)

(b) The Rentiers' Case

We will show the lower semi-continuity of the mapping (12.vii) defined for each $(P, y^1, y^2, \ldots, y^\mu) \in S^* \times \Xi$. Again we have only to find at least one feasible solution $x^i \in B^i$ such that :

(i) x^i satisfies, except for the last equality, the set of budget constraints (2.ii)" in strict inequality,

(ii) x^i satisfies the set of money constraints (2.ii.a)' in strict inequality, and

(iii) x^i satisfies the inequalities (2.ii.b) not necessarily in strict inequality.

For rentiers, the most difficult case of finding such an x^i in that where the i-th rentier corresponds to a) or b) on 68-69 above,[163] and where, at the same time, the elements of vector $P \in S^*$, other than $P_{o,1}$ and $P_{o,n+1}$, are all zero. For this case, we will show, by example, that such an x^i can be found for $(P_{o,1},0,0,\ldots, P_{o,n+1},0,y^1,y^2, \ldots, y^\mu) \in S^* \times \Xi$, where S^* is the set defined in (12.i) or (12.ii).

First, from Assumption VIII.1.a), b) and Assumption II.2, we can suppose that the i-th rentier expects to receive a positive dividend in at least one period, say, only the 2nd period. That is, we can suppose that $\sum_{k=1}^{\mu}\alpha^i_{2,k}\pi^i_{2,k} > 0$ and $\sum_{k=1}^{\mu}\alpha^i_{t,k}\pi^i_{t,k} = 0$ $(t=0,1,3, \ldots, \tau)$, without loss of generality.

Second, suppose that the elements of $P \in S^*$ (other than $P_{o,1}$ and $P_{o,n+1}$) are zero, $x^i_{o,o} = x^i_{1,o} = 0$, $x^i_{t,n+1}(t=0,1,2) \leqq 0$, $x^i_{t,n+1}(t=3,4, \ldots, \tau-1) = 0$, and $x^i_{t,j} = 0$ $(t=0,1, \ldots, \tau;\ j=1,2, \ldots, n)$. Then, our budget constraints (2.ii)" and our money constraints (2.ii.a)' are written as follows :

$$P_{o,n+1}x^i_{o,n+1} \leqq 0$$

$$P^i_{1,n+1}x^i_{1,n+1} \leqq x^i_{o,n+1}$$

$$\text{(2.ii)"} \quad P^i_{2,n+1}x^i_{2,n+1} + x^i_{2,o} \leqq x^i_{1,n+1} + \sum_{k=1}^{\mu}\alpha^i_{2,k}\pi^i_{2,k}$$

$$x^i_{3,o} \leqq x^i_{2,n+1} + x^i_{2,o}$$

---

163. Cf. Assumption IV.9 on p. 26 above.

$$x^i_{4,o} \leqq x^i_{3,o}$$
$$\vdots$$
$$0 \leqq x^i_{\tau-1,o}.$$

$$0 \leqq -\kappa^i_{o,n+1} P_{o,n+1} x^i_{o,n+1}$$

$$- x^i_{o,n+1} \leqq -\kappa^i_{1,n+1} P^i_{1,n+1} x^i_{1,n+1}$$

$$- x^i_{1,n+1} \leqq -\kappa^i_{2,n+1} P^i_{2,n+1} x^i_{2,n+1}$$

$$\text{(2.ii.a)}' \qquad - x^i_{2,n+1} \leqq x^i_{2,o}$$

$$0 \leqq x^i_{3,o}$$

$$0 \leqq x^i_{4,o}$$
$$\vdots$$
$$0 \leqq x^i_{\tau-1,o}.$$

From these inequalities (2.ii)" and (2.ii.a)', taking into account the fact that $\kappa^i_{t,n+1}(t=0,1,2)$, $P_{o,n+1}$, and $P^i_{t,n+1}(t=1,2)$ are positive,[164] we can show an example of a solution which satisfies the set of inequalities (2.ii.a)', as well as (2.ii)", in strict inequality.

Third, an example of such a solution x^i can be found through the following procedure. Consider the inequalities (α) and (β) :

$$(\alpha) \qquad 0 < x^i_{2,n+1} + x^i_{2,o} \leqq P^i_{2,n+1} x^i_{2,n+1} + x^i_{2,o} < \sum_{k=1}^{\mu} \alpha^i_{2,k} \pi^i_{2,k}$$

$$(\beta) \qquad x^i_{2,n+1} < 0 \text{ and } x^i_{2,o} > 0.$$

It is evident that a solution $(x^i_{2,n+1}, x^i_{2,o})$ which satisfies (α) and (β) can be easily found. Next, let $x^i_{1,n+1}$ be some negative number sufficiently small in absolute

---

164. Cf. Assumption IV.9 on p. 26 and Assumption VIII.1 on p. 30 above.

value such that, for this $(x^i_{2,n+1}, x^i_{2,o})$, $x^i_{1,n+1}$ satisfies the following inequalities (γ) and (δ) :

$$(\gamma) \qquad p^i_{2,n+1}x^i_{2,n+1} + x^i_{2,o} < x^i_{1,n+1} + \sum_{k=1}^{\mu}\alpha^i_{2,k}\pi^i_{2,k}$$

$$(\delta) \qquad - x^i_{1,n+1} < - \kappa^i_{2,n+1}p^i_{2,n+1}x^i_{2,n+1}.$$

Finally, as will be easily seen, there exists at least one feasible solution x^i, belonging to B^i, which satisfies (2.ii)" and (2.ii.a)' in strict inequality. It satisfies, as well, the inequalities (2.ii.b), not necessarily in strict inequality. For example, there is a solution $(x^i_{o,n+1} < 0,\ x^i_{o,o} = 0,\ x^i_{1,n+1} < 0,\ x^i_{1,o} = 0,\ x^i_{2,n+1} < 0,\ x^i_{2,o} > 0,\ x^i_{3,n+1} = 0,\ x^i_{3,o} > 0,\ \ldots\ldots\ldots\ldots)$ where $x^i_{t,n+1}(t=3,4, \ldots, \tau-1) = 0$, $x^i_{t,o}(t=3,4, \ldots, \tau-1) > 0$, and $x^i_{t,j}(t=0,1, \ldots, \tau;\ j=1,2, \ldots, n)$ is zero.

Again, for the complete proof of lower semi-continuity after finding such a feasible solution x^i, see Haga and Otsuki's article mentioned above, together with Appendix III of the present article.

(c) The Firms' Case

We will show below the lower semi-continuity of the mapping (10.iii) defined for each $P \in S^{\bar{\mathfrak{n}}}$. The right-hand side of the first inequality of (3)' takes some positive value, due to Assumption II.3 and the positivity of prices. Moreover, the right-hand side of the first inequality of (3.a)' takes some positive value, due to Assumption IV.6. Hence, if we let the elements $y^k_{t,o}(t=0,1, \ldots, \tau-1)$ of vector y^k be respectively appropriate positive numbers and let all other elements of y^k be zero, then we can find a feasible solution $y^k \in A^k$ such that :

(i) y^k satisfies (3)' in strict inequality,

(ii) y^k satisfies (3.a)' in strict inequality,

(iii) y^k satisfies (3.b) and (3.c) not necessarily in strict inequality, and

(iv) y^k satisfies (3.d) in strict inequality.

Again, refer to Haga and Otsuki's article, as mentioned above, together with Appendix III, for the complete proof of lower semi-continuity after findind such a solution y^k.

APPENDIX III

(1) We will prove below that the sets of feasible solutions of the non-linear inequalities (2.i.a)', (2.ii.a)', and (3.a)' are convex sets. However, only the essentials of the proof will be presented. For convenience, notations other than those of the above text are employed. For example, $\kappa^{i}_{t,j}$, $\kappa^{i}_{t,n+1}$, $\kappa^{i}_{t,b}$, *etc.*, are all denoted by the same letter, κ.

Now, suppose that x and y are two different solutions which satisfy, respectively, the following inequalities :

1) $\max\{(x-a),0\} - \kappa \max\{(a-x),0\} \leqq C,$

2) $\max\{(y-a),0\} - \kappa \max\{(a-y),0\} \leqq C,$

where $0 \leqq \kappa \leqq 1$, a and C are constant.

For the purpose of proof, it is sufficient if we show that the following inequality holds :

$$\text{(I)}\quad \max[\{(\alpha x + \beta y) - a\},0] - \kappa \max[\{a - (\alpha x + \beta y)\},0]$$
$$\leqq \alpha[\max\{(x-a),0\} - \kappa \max\{(a-x),0\}] + \beta[\max\{(y-a),0\}$$
$$- \kappa \max\{(a-y),0\}] \leqq C,$$

where $\alpha \geqq 0$, $\beta \geqq 0$, and $\alpha + \beta = 1$.

For simplicity, let A denote the first expression of (I), *i.e.* $\max[\{(\alpha x + \beta y)- a\},0] - \kappa \max[\{a - (\alpha x + \beta y)\},0]$ and let B denote the second expression, *i.e.* $\alpha[\max\{(x-a),0\} - \kappa \max\{(a-x),0\}] + \beta[\max\{(y-a),0\} - \kappa \max\{(a-y),0\}]$.

We will show that the inequality (I) holds in all possible cases i),ii),iii), iv),v) and vi).

i) In the case where $x \geqq a$, $y \leqq a$, and $\alpha x + \beta y - a \geqq 0$, then

$$B - A = \alpha(1 - \kappa)(a - y) \geqq 0.$$

Thus (I) holds.

ii) In the case where $x \geqq a$, $y \leqq a$, and $\alpha x + \beta y - a < 0$, then

$$B - A \geqq 0.$$

Thus (I) holds.

iii) In the case where $x \leqq a$ and $y \leqq a$, then necessarily

$\alpha x + \beta y - a \leqq 0$, and

$$B - A \geqq 0.$$

Thus (I) holds.

iv) In the case where $x \geqq a$ and $y \geqq a$, then necessarily

$\alpha x + \beta y - a \geqq 0$, and

$$B - A = 0.$$

Thus (I) holds.

v) In the case where $x \leqq a \leqq y$ and $\alpha x + \beta y - a \geqq 0$, then

$$B - A = \beta(1 - \kappa)(a - x) \geqq 0.$$

Thus (I) holds.

vi) Finally, in the case where $x \leqq a \leqq y$ and $\alpha x + \beta y - a < 0$, then

$$B - A = \alpha(1 - \kappa)(y - a) \geqq 0.$$

Thus (I) holds in case vi), as well. This completes the essential proof that the feasible solutions of the non-linear inequalities (2.i.a)',(2.ii.a)' and (3.a)' are convex sets.

(2) We can see that if i)' and ii)' hold, then necessarily, the following (I)' holds. That is,

i)' $\max\{(x - a),0\} - \kappa \max\{(a - x),0\} \leqq C.$

ii)' $\max\{(y - a),0\} - \quad \max\{(a - y),0\} < C.$

As a result of the preceding discussion (I)',

(I)' $\max[\{(\alpha x + \beta y) - a\},0] - \kappa \max[\{a - (\alpha x + \beta y)\},0] < C.$

APPENDIX IV

From Assumption IV.10, there is at least one rentier i for whom $\kappa^i_{t,b} = 1 (t=0,1, \ldots, \tau-1)$. We will show that, if the price of bonds in the 0-th period $P_{o,n+1}$ is zero, the rentier's demand for such bonds will increase without limit, *i.e.* $x^i_{o,n+1} = \infty$. Although at first glance this conclusion seems to be self-evident, it is not so simple, because our model differs from usual models in that it contains the set of money constraints (2.ii.a)' and the set of other constraints (2.ii.b) originating in Assumption V.3. However, we can verify this conclusion by making use of some other assumptions given in our model.

It is clear that, among the inequalities (2.ii.b), $x^i_{o,n+1} - x^i_{1,n+1} \leqq \Delta$ is satisfied with strict equality, due to the rentier's maximization behaviour. The rentier increases $x^i_{o,n+1}$ as long as $x^i_{o,n+1} - x^i_{1,n+1} < \Delta$. If $x^i_{1,n+1}$ is left unchanged, the moment that the inequality $x^i_{o,n+1} - x^i_{1,n+1} \leqq \Delta$ is violated he will stop increasing $x^i_{o,n+1}$. However, if, keeping the equality $x^i_{o,n+1} - x^i_{1,n+1} = \Delta$, the rentier can increase $x^i_{1,n+1}$ as well as $x^i_{o,n+1}$, then he increases $x^i_{o,n+1}$ without limit. That is, such an increase of demand follows because, if $P_{o,n+1} = 0$, an increase of $x^i_{o,n+1}$ does not violate the budget constraint in the 0-th period of (2.ii)" or (2.ii)' and, at the same time, it increases the value of the right-hand side of the budget constraint in the 1st period. That is, because of the increase of this value, the rentier expands his purchases of real goods on and after the 1st period in order to increase his utility.

But, although we have discussed such an increase of demand for bonds only in relation to the budget constraints (2.ii)" or (2.ii)', the question is whether such an increase of $x^i_{o,n+1}$ does not violate (2.ii.a)' as well.

To investigate this problem, first examine the second inequality of the money constraints (2.ii.a)' in all possible cases of bond demand or supply:[165]

(i) $x^i_{o,n+1} \geqq 0$ (ii) $x^i_{o,n+1} \geqq 0$

$x^i_{1,n+1} \leqq 0$ $x^i_{1,n+1} \geqq 0$

(iii) $x^i_{o,n+1} \leqq 0$ (iv) $x^i_{o,n+1} \leqq 0$

$x^i_{1,n+1} \leqq 0$ $x^i_{1,n+1} \geqq 0$.

Corresponding to these cases, the following cases (i)',(ii)',(iii)', and (iv)' must hold respectively for the second inequality of (2.ii.a)'. In order to simplify notation, the subscript i of $x^i_{o,n+1}$, $P^i_{1,n+1}$, $\kappa^i_{o,b}$, *etc.* will be omitted :

$$\text{(i)'} \quad \sum_{j=2}^{n} P_{1,j}x_{1,j} \leqq x_{o,o} + \kappa_{o,b}x_{o,n+1} - \kappa_{1,n+1}P_{1,n+1}x_{1,n+1}.$$

$$\text{(ii)'} \quad \sum_{j=2}^{n} P_{1,j}x_{1,j} + P_{1,n+1}x_{1,n+1} \leqq x_{o,o} + \kappa_{o,b}x_{o,n+1}.$$

$$\text{(iii)'} \quad \sum_{j=2}^{n} P_{1,j}x_{1,j} \leqq x_{o,o} + \max(\kappa_{o,b}x_{o,n+1},0) - \kappa_{1,n+1}P_{1,n+1}x_{1,n+1} + x_{o,n+1}.$$

$$\text{(iv)'} \quad \sum_{j=2}^{n} P_{1,j}x_{1,j} \leqq x_{o,o} + \max(\kappa_{o,b}x_{o,n+1},0) - P_{1,n+1}x_{1,n+1} + x_{o,n+1}.$$

In these four inequalities, if variables other than $x_{o,n+1}$ are kept constant, then $x_{o,n+1}$ increases without limit, because $\kappa_{o,b} = 1$.

However, we must consider the constraint $x_{o,n+1} - x_{1,n+1} \leqq \Delta$ for the money constraints as well as for the budget constraints. Again, the rentier can continue to increase $x_{o,n+1}$, and does not stop increasing it as long as $x_{o,n+1} - x_{1,n+1} < \Delta$, because he can increase his utility by doing so.

---

165. We need not treat the first inequality of (2.ii.a)' because $P_{o,n+1} = 0$.

Therefore, a necessary condition for the rentier's maximization behaviour is the following (A) :

$$\text{(A)} \qquad x_{o,n+1} - x_{1,n+1} = \Delta.$$

The question comes back to whether or not we can increase $x_{o,n+1}$ without limit, subject to (A), (2.ii)', and (2.ii.a)'.

Now, taking into account (A), the second inequality of (2.ii)" or (2.ii)' is the following (B) :

$$\text{(B)} \qquad \sum_{j=2}^{n} P_{1,j}x_{1,j} + x_{1,o} \leqq (1 - P_{1,n+1})x_{o,n+1} + P_{1,n+1}\Delta$$
$$+ x_{o,o} + \sum_{k=1}^{\mu}\alpha_{1,k}\pi_{1,k} = (1 - P_{1,n+1})x_{1,n+1} + \Delta$$
$$+ x_{o,o} + \sum_{k=1}^{\mu}\alpha_{1,k}\pi_{1,k}.$$

Here, $(1 - P_{1,n+1})$ is positive by virtue of Assumption VIII.2 and the fact that $P_{o,n+1} = 0$. Hence we can infinitely increase $x_{o,n+1}$ without violating (B). Also, as long as (A) and the inequality $x_{1,n+1} - x_{2,n+1} \leqq \Delta$ hold, the rentier can increase $x_{1,n+1}$ as well as $x_{o,n+1}$ without limit. This is because, as is the case with an increase of $x_{o,n+1}$, an increase of $x_{1,n+1}$ increases the value of the right-hand side of the budget constraint in the 2nd period as well (Cf. the inequality (C)). Consequently, the rentier can expand his purchases of real goods on and after the 2nd period to increase his utility. Therefore, he continues to increase $x_{1,n+1}$. Thus, again, a necessary condition for the rentier's maximization is the following (A)' :

$$\text{(A)'} \qquad x_{1,n+1} - x_{2,n+1} = \Delta.$$

Next, the third inequality of (2.ii)" or (2.ii)' becomes, by virtue of (A) and (A)', the following (C) :

$$\text{(C)} \qquad \sum_{j=2}^{n} P_{2,j}x_{2,j} + x_{2,o} \leqq (1 - P_{2,n+1})x_{1,n+1}$$
$$+ P_{1,n+1}\Delta + x_{1,o} + \sum_{k=1}^{\mu}\alpha_{2,k}\pi_{2,k}$$

$$= (1 - P_{2,n+1})x_{2,n+1} + \Delta + x_{1,o} + \sum_{k=1}^{\mu}\alpha_{2,k}\pi_{2,k}.$$

Since $(1 - P_{2,n+1})$ is positive by virtue of Assumption VIII.2, this inequality is not violated hoerver much $x_{o,n+1}$ and $x_{1,n+1}$ are increased under equalities (A) and (A)'. Thus, if $P_{o,n+1} = 0$, then $x_{o,n+1}$ increases without limit, as long as the equalities (A) and (A)' hold.

Now, the four inequalities derived from the second inequality of money constraints (2.ii.a)', *i.e.*, (i)',(ii)',(iii)' and (iv)', were formulated from (2.ii.a)', independently of constraints (2.ii.b). However, since (A) is a necessary condition, we must formulate and examine the second inequality of (2.ii.a)', taking into account the equality (A). Thus,

$$\text{(D)} \quad \sum_{j=2}^{n}P_{1,j}x_{1,j} + \max\{P_{1,n+1}(x_{o,n+1} - \Delta),0\}$$
$$+ \max(-x_{o,n+1},0) \leqq x_{o,o} + \max(\kappa_{o,b}x_{o,n+1},0)$$
$$+ \max\{-\kappa_{1,n+1}P_{1,n+1}(x_{o,n+1} - \Delta),0\}.$$

For clarity, we will take up the following three cases :

$$\text{((i))} \quad x_{o,n+1} \leqq 0 \qquad\qquad \text{((ii))} \quad x_{o,n+1} > 0$$
$$x_{o,n+1} - \Delta < 0, \qquad\qquad x_{o,n+1} - \Delta \leqq 0,$$

$$\text{((iii))} \quad x_{o,n+1} > 0$$
$$x_{o,n+1} - \Delta \geqq 0.$$

These cases cover all possibilities.

Now, corresponding to ((i)), ((ii)), and ((iii)), (D) becomes respectively ((i))', ((ii))', and ((iii))' :

$$\text{((i))'} \quad \sum_{j=2}^{n}P_{1,j}x_{1,j} \leqq x_{o,o} + \max(\kappa_{o,b}x_{o,n+1},0)$$
$$+ (1 - \kappa_{1,n+1}P_{1,n+1})x_{o,n+1} + \Delta\kappa_{1,n+1}P_{1,n+1} = x_{o,o}$$
$$+ \max\{\kappa_{o,b}(\Delta + x_{1,n+1}),0\} + (1 - \kappa_{1,n+1}P_{1,n+1})x_{1,n+1} + \Delta.$$

$$((ii))' \quad \sum_{j=2}^{n} P_{1,j}x_{1,j} \leqq x_{o,o} + (\kappa_{o,b} - \kappa_{1,n+1}P_{1,n+1})x_{o,n+1}$$

$$\Delta\kappa_{1,n+1}P_{1,n+1} = x_{o,o} + (\kappa_{o,b} - \kappa_{1,n+1}P_{1,n+1})x_{1,n+1} + \Delta\kappa_{o,b}.$$

$$((iii))' \quad \sum_{j=2}^{n} P_{1,j}x_{1,j} \leqq x_{o,o} + (\kappa_{o,b} - P_{1,n+1})x_{o,n+1} + \Delta P_{1,n+1} = x_{o,o}$$

$$+ (\kappa_{o,b} - P_{1,n+1})x_{1,n+1} + \Delta\kappa_{o,b}.$$

In these inequalities, we can conclude that $x_{o,n+1}$ increases without limit. This conclusion necessarily follows because $(1 - \kappa_{1,n+1}P_{1,n+1}) > 0$, $(\kappa_{o,b} - \kappa_{1,n+1}P_{1,n+1}) > 0$, and $(\kappa_{o,b} - P_{1,n+1}) > 0$.[166] Also, we see that, as long as (A) and (A)' hold, the rentier can increase $x_{1,n+1}$ as well as $x_{o,n+1}$ without limit.

Also, regarding the third and subsequent inequalities of (2.ii.a)', we can draw the same conclusion. Though the procedure for the third inequality should be obvious, for the sake of completeness we will describe the main points of the proof. That is, the third inequality of (2.ii.a)' becomes the following (E) :

$$(E) \quad \sum_{j=2}^{n} P_{2,j}x_{2,j} + \max(P_{2,n+1}x_{2,n+1},0) + \max(-x_{1,n+1},0)$$

$$\leqq x_{1,o} + \max(\kappa_{1,b}x_{1,n+1},0) + \max(-\kappa_{2,n+1}P_{2,n+1}x_{2,n+1},0).$$

Let us formulate and examine the inequality (E), separately, in the four possible case (i)',(ii)',(iii)', and (iv)', which, as we have seen, are based on (i), (ii),(iii), and (iv).

Next, taking into account the necessary condition, $x_{1,n+1} - x_{2,n+1} = \Delta$, reformulate (E) as we did (D). Then, examine (E) according to the same procedures by which ((i))', ((ii))', and ((iii))' were formulated, corresponding to ((i)), ((ii)) and ((iii)) of (D).

If we continue the same procedure successively, we see that since, and as long as, we can continue to keep the equality $x_{t,n+1} - x_{t+1,n+1} = \Delta$ by increasing

---

166. See Assumption IV.4.c), Assumption IV.10, and Assumption VIII.2.

$x_{t+1,n+1}$ by the same amount as $x_{t,n+1}$, both $x_{t,n+1}$ and $x_{t+1,n+1}$ $(t=0,1, \ldots, \tau-2)$ can increase without limit. Therefore we can conclude that, for a rentier coming under Assumption IV.10, if $P_{o,n+1} = 0$, then $x_{o,n+1} = \infty$, subject to the entire set of budget constraints (2.ii)" or (2.ii)', the entire set of money constraints (2.ii.a)', and the entire set of other constraints (2.ii.b).[167]

167. In both (2.ii)" and (2.ii.a)', the last inequalities differ from the other inequalities. However, our procedure is more easily applied to the last inequalities.

REFERENCES

[1] Berge, C., *Topological Spaces*, translated by E.M. Patterson, Edinburgh and London: Oliver & Boyd, 1963.

[2] Clower, R.W., "The Keynesian Counter-Revolution: A Theoretical Appraisal", ch. 5 of *The Theory of Interest Rates*, edited by F.H. Hahn and F. Brechling, International Economic Association Series, London: Macmillan, 1965, pp. 103-125, or in *Monetary Theory*, edited by R.W. Clower, Penguin Modern Economics Readings, 1969, pp. 270-297.

[3] Dieudonné, J., *Foundations of Modern Analysis*, New York and London: Academic Press, 1969.

[4] Glustoff, E., "On the Existence of a Keynesian Equilibrium", *Review of Economic Studies*, vol. 35, No. 103, (July, 1968), pp. 327-334.

[5] Grandmont, J.M. and Y. Younes, "On the Role of Money and the Existence of a Monetary Equilibrium", *Review of Economic Studies*, vol. 39, (1972), pp. 149-165.

[6] Haga, H., "Kahei to Ippan-Kinko ni Kansuru Saikosatsu" (Reconsideration of Money and General Equilibrium), *Keizai-Gaku* (Tohoku University), vol. 31, No. 4, (1970).

[7] Haga, H., "Kahei to Ippan-Kinko Riron" (Money and General Equilibrium), in *Gendai-Keizaigaku no Tenkai (Contemporary Economic Analysis — Survey and Extension —)*, edited by M. Kaji and Y. Murakami, Tokyo: Keiso-shobo, 1971, pp. 3-27.

[8] Haga, H., "Keynes no Kashokoyo-Kinko ni tsuite" (On the Under-Employment Equilibrium of Keynes), Tohoku Economics Research Group (TERG) Discussion Paper, No. 10, 1973.

[9] Haga, H., "Keynes no Kashokoyo-Kinko Taikei no Kahei to Shoken o hukumu Walras teki Taikei ni yoru Saikosatsu" (Reconsideration of Keynes' Under-Employment Equilibrium System by the Walrasian System including Money and Bonds), *Keizai-Gaku* (Tohoku University), vol. 36, No. 2, (1974).

[10] Haga, H., and M. Otsuki, "On a Generalized von Neumann Model", *International Economic Review*, vol. 6, (1965), pp. 115-123.

[11] Intriligator, M.D., *Mathematical Optimization and Economic Theory*, Englewood Cliffs, N.J.: Prentice-Hall, 1971.

[12] Kakutani, S., "A Generalization of Brouwer's Fixed Point Theorem", *Duke Mathematical Journal*, vol. 8, (1941), pp. 457-459.

[13] Keynes, J.M., *The General Theory of Employment, Interest and Money*, London: Macmillan, 1936.

[14] Leijonhufvud, A., *On Keynesian Economics and the Economics of Keynes*, New York: Oxford University Press, 1968.

[15] Morishima, M., *Shihonshugi-Keizai no Hendo-Riron (Theory of Economic Fluctu-*

ation in a Capitalist Economy), Tokyo: Sobun-sha, 1958.

[16] Negishi, T., "Kahei no Ippan-Kinko Bunseki" (General Equilibrium in a Monetary Economy — Existence and Dichotomy —), *Journal of Economics* (Tokyo University), vol. 32, (1966).

[17] Nikaido, H., *Introduction to Sets and Mappings in Modern Economics*, Amsterdam: North-Holland, 1970.

[18] Nikaido, H., *Convex Structures and Economic Theory*, New York: Academic Press, 1968.

[19] Ohlin, B., "Some Notes on the Stockholm Theory of Savings and Investment", *Economic Journal*, vol. 47, No. 185-186, (1937), pp. 35-69, pp. 221-240.

[20] Okumura, R., "Torihiki-Hiyo to Kaheiteki-Kinko" (Transaction Cost and Monetary Equilibrium), *Keizai-Gaku* (Tohoku University), vol. 37, No. 1, (1975).

[21] Patinkin, D., "Liquidity Preference and Loanable Funds", *Economica*, vol. 25, (1958), pp. 300-318.

[22] Patinkin, D., *Money, Interest, and Prices*, 2nd ed., New York: Harper & Row, 1965.

[23] Solow, R.M., "Competitive Valuation in a Dynamic Input-Output System", *Econometrica*, vol. 27, No. 1, (1959), pp. 30-53.

[24] Walras, L., *Elements of Pure Economics*, translated by W. Jaffé, London: Allen and Unwin, (1954), (English translation of the definitive edition of *Éléments d'économie politique pure*).

Vol. 59: J. A. Hanson, Growth in Open Economies. V, 128 pages. 1971.

Vol. 60: H. Hauptmann, Schätz- und Kontrolltheorie in stetigen dynamischen Wirtschaftsmodellen. V, 104 Seiten. 1971.

Vol. 61: K. H. F. Meyer, Wartesysteme mit variabler Bearbeitungsrate. VII, 314 Seiten. 1971.

Vol. 62: W. Krelle u. G. Gabisch unter Mitarbeit von J. Burgermeister, Wachstumstheorie. VII, 223 Seiten. 1972.

Vol. 63: J. Kohlas, Monte Carlo Simulation im Operations Research. VI, 162 Seiten. 1972.

Vol. 64: P. Gessner u. K. Spremann, Optimierung in Funktionenräumen. IV, 120 Seiten. 1972.

Vol. 65: W. Everling, Exercises in Computer Systems Analysis. VIII, 184 pages. 1972.

Vol. 66: F. Bauer, P. Garabedian and D. Korn, Supercritical Wing Sections. V, 211 pages. 1972.

Vol. 67: I. V. Girsanov, Lectures on Mathematical Theory of Extremum Problems. V, 136 pages. 1972.

Vol. 68: J. Loeckx, Computability and Decidability. An Introduction for Students of Computer Science. VI, 76 pages. 1972.

Vol. 69: S. Ashour, Sequencing Theory. V, 133 pages. 1972.

Vol. 70: J. P. Brown, The Economic Effects of Floods. Investigations of a Stochastic Model of Rational Investment. Behavior in the Face of Floods. V, 87 pages. 1972.

Vol. 71: R. Henn und O. Opitz, Konsum- und Produktionstheorie II. V, 134 Seiten. 1972.

Vol. 72: T. P. Bagchi and J. G. C. Templeton, Numerical Methods in Markov Chains and Bulk Queues. XI, 89 pages. 1972.

Vol. 73: H. Kiendl, Suboptimale Regler mit abschnittweise linearer Struktur. VI, 146 Seiten. 1972.

Vol. 74: F. Pokropp, Aggregation von Produktionsfunktionen. VI, 107 Seiten. 1972.

Vol. 75: GI-Gesellschaft für Informatik e.V. Bericht Nr. 3. 1. Fachtagung über Programmiersprachen · München, 9.–11. März 1971. Herausgegeben im Auftrag der Gesellschaft für Informatik von H. Langmaack und M. Paul. VII, 280 Seiten. 1972.

Vol. 76: G. Fandel, Optimale Entscheidung bei mehrfacher Zielsetzung. II, 121 Seiten. 1972.

Vol. 77: A. Auslender, Problèmes de Minimax via l'Analyse Convexe et les Inégalités Variationelles: Théorie et Algorithmes. VII, 132 pages. 1972.

Vol. 78: GI-Gesellschaft für Informatik e.V. 2. Jahrestagung, Karlsruhe, 2.–4. Oktober 1972. Herausgegeben im Auftrag der Gesellschaft für Informatik von P. Deussen. XI, 576 Seiten. 1973.

Vol. 79: A. Berman, Cones, Matrices and Mathematical Programming. V, 96 pages. 1973.

Vol. 80: International Seminar on Trends in Mathematical Modelling, Venice, 13–18 December 1971. Edited by N. Hawkes. VI, 288 pages. 1973.

Vol. 81: Advanced Course on Software Engineering. Edited by F. L. Bauer. XII, 545 pages. 1973.

Vol. 82: R. Saeks, Resolution Space, Operators and Systems. X, 267 pages. 1973.

Vol. 83: NTG/GI-Gesellschaft für Informatik, Nachrichtentechnische Gesellschaft. Fachtagung „Cognitive Verfahren und Systeme", Hamburg, 11.–13. April 1973. Herausgegeben im Auftrag der NTG/GI von Th. Einsele, W. Giloi und H.-H. Nagel. VIII, 373 Seiten. 1973.

Vol. 84: A. V. Balakrishnan, Stochastic Differential Systems I. Filtering and Control. A Function Space Approach. V, 252 pages. 1973.

Vol. 85: T. Page, Economics of Involuntary Transfers: A Unified Approach to Pollution and Congestion Externalities. XI, 159 pages. 1973.

Vol. 86: Symposium on the Theory of Scheduling and its Applications. Edited by S. E. Elmaghraby. VIII, 437 pages. 1973.

Vol. 87: G. F. Newell, Approximate Stochastic Behavior of n-Server Service Systems with Large n. VII, 118 pages. 1973.

Vol. 88: H. Steckhan, Güterströme in Netzen. VII, 134 Seiten. 1973.

Vol. 89: J. P. Wallace and A. Sherret, Estimation of Product. Attributes and Their Importances. V, 94 pages. 1973.

Vol. 90: J.-F. Richard, Posterior and Predictive Densities for Simultaneous Equation Models. VI, 226 pages. 1973.

Vol. 91: Th. Marschak and R. Selten, General Equilibrium with Price-Making Firms. XI, 246 pages. 1974.

Vol. 92: E. Dierker, Topological Methods in Walrasian Economics. IV, 130 pages. 1974.

Vol. 93: 4th IFAC/IFIP International Conference on Digital Computer Applications to Process Control, Part I. Zürich/Switzerland, March 19–22, 1974. Edited by M. Mansour and W. Schaufelberger. XVIII, 544 pages. 1974.

Vol. 94: 4th IFAC/IFIP International Conference on Digital Computer Applications to Process Control, Part II. Zürich/Switzerland, March 19–22, 1974. Edited by M. Mansour and W. Schaufelberger. XVIII, 546 pages. 1974.

Vol. 95: M. Zeleny, Linear Multiobjective Programming. X, 220 pages. 1974.

Vol. 96: O. Moeschlin, Zur Theorie von Neumannscher Wachstumsmodelle. XI, 115 Seiten. 1974.

Vol. 97: G. Schmidt, Über die Stabilität des einfachen Bedienungskanals. VII, 147 Seiten. 1974.

Vol. 98: Mathematical Methods in Queueing Theory. Proceedings 1973. Edited by A. B. Clarke. VII, 374 pages. 1974.

Vol. 99: Production Theory. Edited by W. Eichhorn, R. Henn, O. Opitz, and R. W. Shephard. VIII, 386 pages. 1974.

Vol. 100: B. S. Duran and P. L. Odell, Cluster Analysis. A Survey. VI, 137 pages. 1974.

Vol. 101: W. M. Wonham, Linear Multivariable Control. A Geometric Approach. X, 344 pages. 1974.

Vol. 102: Analyse Convexe et Ses Applications. Comptes Rendus, Janvier 1974. Edited by J.-P. Aubin. IV, 244 pages. 1974.

Vol. 103: D. E. Boyce, A. Farhi, R. Weischedel, Optimal Subset Selection. Multiple Regression, Interdependence and Optimal Network Algorithms. XIII, 187 pages. 1974.

Vol. 104: S. Fujino, A Neo-Keynesian Theory of Inflation and Economic Growth. V, 96 pages. 1974.

Vol. 105: Optimal Control Theory and its Applications. Part I. Proceedings 1973. Edited by B. J. Kirby. VI, 425 pages. 1974.

Vol. 106: Optimal Control Theory and its Applications. Part II. Proceedings 1973. Edited by B. J. Kirby. VI, 403 pages. 1974.

Vol. 107: Control Theory, Numerical Methods and Computer Systems Modeling. International Symposium, Rocquencourt, June 17–21, 1974. Edited by A. Bensoussan and J. L. Lions. VIII, 757 pages. 1975.

Vol. 108: F. Bauer et al., Supercritical Wing Sections II. A Handbook. V, 296 pages. 1975.

Vol. 109: R. von Randow, Introduction to the Theory of Matroids. IX, 102 pages. 1975.

Vol. 110: C. Striebel, Optimal Control of Discrete Time Stochastic Systems. III. 208 pages. 1975.

Vol. 111: Variable Structure Systems with Application to Economics and Biology. Proceedings 1974. Edited by A. Ruberti and R. R. Mohler. VI, 321 pages. 1975.

Vol. 112: J. Wilhlem, Objectives and Multi-Objective Decision Making Under Uncertainty. IV, 111 pages. 1975.

Vol. 113: G. A. Aschinger, Stabilitätsaussagen über Klassen von Matrizen mit verschwindenden Zeilensummen. V, 102 Seiten. 1975.

Vol. 114: G. Uebe, Produktionstheorie. XVII, 301 Seiten. 1976.

Vol. 115: Anderson et al., Foundations of System Theory: Finitary and Infinitary Conditions. VII, 93 pages. 1976

Vol. 116: K. Miyazawa, Input-Output Analysis and the Structure of Income Distribution. IX, 135 pages. 1976.

Vol. 117: Optimization and Operations Research. Proceedings 1975. Edited by W. Oettli and K. Ritter. IV, 316 pages. 1976.

Vol. 118: Traffic Equilibrium Methods, Proceedings 1974. Edited by M. A. Florian. XXIII, 432 pages. 1976.

Vol. 119: Inflation in Small Countries. Proceedings 1974. Edited by H. Frisch. VI, 356 pages. 1976.

Vol. 120: G. Hasenkamp, Specification and Estimation of Multiple-Output Production Functions. VII, 151 pages. 1976.

Vol. 121: J. W. Cohen, On Regenerative Processes in Queueing Theory. IX, 93 pages. 1976.

Vol. 122: M. S. Bazaraa, and C. M. Shetty,Foundations of Optimization VI. 193 pages. 1976

Vol. 123: Multiple Criteria Decision Making. Kyoto 1975. Edited by M. Zeleny. XXVII, 345 pages. 1976.

Vol. 124: M. J. Todd. The Computation of Fixed Points and Applications. VII, 129 pages. 1976.

Vol. 125: Karl C. Mosler. Optimale Transportnetze. Zur Bestimmung ihres kostengünstigsten Standorts bei gegebener Nachfrage. VI, 142 Seiten. 1976.

Vol. 126: Energy, Regional Science and Public Policy. Energy and Environment I. Proceedings 1975. Edited by M. Chatterji and P. Van Rompuy. VIII, 316 pages. 1976.

Vol. 127: Environment, Regional Science and Interregional Modeling. Energy and Environment II. Proceedings 1975. Edited by M. Chatterji and P. Van Rompuy. IX, 211 pages. 1976.

Vol. 128: Integer Programming and Related Areas. A Classified Bibliography. Edited by C. Kastning. XII, 495 pages. 1976.

Vol. 129: H.-J. Lüthi, Komplementaritäts- und Fixpunktalgorithmen in der mathematischen Programmierung. Spieltheorie und Ökonomie. VII, 145 Seiten. 1976.

Vol. 130: Multiple Criteria Decision Making, Jouy-en-Josas, France. Proceedings 1975. Edited by H. Thiriez and S. Zionts. VI, 409 pages. 1976.

Vol. 131: Mathematical Systems Theory. Proceedings 1975. Edited by G. Marchesini and S. K. Mitter. X, 408 pages. 1976.

Vol. 132: U. H. Funke, Mathematical Models in Marketing. A Collection of Abstracts. XX, 514 pages. 1976.

Vol. 133: Warsaw Fall Seminars in Mathematical Economics 1975. Edited by M. W. Loś, J. Loś, and A. Wieczorek. V. 159 pages. 1976.

Vol. 134: Computing Methods in Applied Sciences and Engineering. Proceedings 1975. VII, 390 pages. 1976.

Vol. 135: H. Haga, A Disequilibrium–Equilibrium Model with Money and Bonds. A Keynesian–Walrasian Synthesis. VI, 119 pages. 1976.

Ökonometrie und Unternehmensforschung
Econometrics and Operations Research

Vol. I	Nichtlineare Programmierung. Von H. P. Künzi und W. Krelle unter Mitwirkung von W. Oettli. Vergriffen
Vol. II	Lineare Programmierung und Erweiterungen. Von G. B. Dantzig. Ins Deutsche übertragen und bearbeitet von A. Jaeger. – Mit 103 Abbildungen. XVI, 712 Seiten. 1966. Geb.
Vol. III	Stochastic Processes. By M. Girault. – With 35 figures. XII, 126 pages. 1966. Cloth
Vol. IV	Methoden der Unternehmensforschung im Versicherungswesen. Von K. H. Wolff. – Mit 14 Diagrammen. VIII, 266 Seiten. 1966. Geb.
Vol. V	The Theory of Max-Min and its Application to Weapons Allocation Problems. By John M. Danskin. – With 6 figures. X, 126 pages. 1967. Cloth
Vol. VI	Entscheidungskriterien bei Risiko. Von H. Schneeweiss. – Mit 35 Abbildungen. XII, 215 Seiten. 1967. Geb.
Vol. VII	Boolean Methods in Operations Research and Related Areas. By P. L. Hammer (Ivănescu) and S. Rudeanu. With a preface by R. Bellman. – With 25 figures. XVI, 329 pages. 1968. Cloth
Vol. VIII	Strategy for R & D: Studies in the Microeconomics of Development. By Th. Marschak. Th K. Glennan Jr., and R. Summers. – With 44 figures. XIV, 330 pages. 1967. Cloth
Vol. IX	Dynamic Programming of Economic Decisions. By M. J. Beckmann. – With 9 figures XII, 143 pages. 1968. Cloth
Vol. X	Input-Output-Analyse. Von J. Schumann. – Mit 12 Abbildungen. X, 311 Seiten. 1968. Geb.
Vol. XI	Produktionstheorie. Von W. Wittmann. – Mit 54 Abbildungen. VIII, 177 Seiten. 1968. Geb.
Vol. XII	Sensitivitätsanalysen und parametrische Programmierung. Von W. Dinkelbach. – Mit 20 Abbildungen. XI, 190 Seiten. 1969. Geb.
Vol. XIII	Graphentheoretische Methoden und ihre Anwendungen. Von W. Knödel. – Mit 24 Abbildungen. VIII, 111 Seiten. 1969. Geb.
Vol. XIV	Praktische Studien zur Unternehmensforschung. Von E. Nievergelt, O. Müller, F. E. Schlaepfer und W. H. Landis. – Mit 82 Abbildungen. XII, 240 Seiten. 1970. Geb.
Vol. XV	Optimale Reihenfolgen. Von H. Müller-Merbach. – Mit 45 Abbildungen. IX, 225 Seiten. 1970. Geb.
Vol. XVI	Preispolitik der Mehrproduktenunternehmung in der statischen Theorie. Von R. Selten. – Mit 20 Abbildungen. VIII, 195 Seiten. 1970. Geb.
Vol. XVII	Information Theory for Systems Engineers. By L. P. Hyvärinen. – With 42 figures. VIII, 197 pages. 1970. Cloth
Vol. XVIII	Unternehmensforschung im Bergbau. Von F. L. Wilke. – Mit 29 Abbildungen. VIII, 150 Seiten. 1972. Geb.
Vol. XIX	Anti-Äquilibrium. Von J. Kornai. – Mit 31 Abbildungen. XVI, 382 Seiten. 1975. Geb.
Vol. XX	Mathematische Optimierung. Von E. Blum, W. Oettli. IX, 413 Seiten. (davon 75 Seiten Bibliographie). 1975. Geb.
Vol. XXI	Stochastic Linear Programming. By P. Kall. VI, 95 pages. 1976. Cloth.

GPSR Compliance

The European Union's (EU) General Product Safety Regulation (GPSR) is a set of rules that requires consumer products to be safe and our obligations to ensure this.

If you have any concerns about our products, you can contact us on ProductSafety@springernature.com

In case Publisher is established outside the EU, the EU authorized representative is:

Springer Nature Customer Service Center GmbH
Europaplatz 3
69115 Heidelberg, Germany

Batch number: 10844827

Printed by Printforce, the Netherlands